商务英语写作
（第2版）

房玉靖 马国志 主 编
鞠媛媛 王 琪 董 陶 副主编

清华大学出版社
北 京

内容简介

本书是作者实地调研了近两年涉外企事业单位对商务助理、文员等岗位能力的需求，结合高等职业院校学生的学习特点，依据我国高等职业院校商务英语专业的培养目标和教学需要而编写的一部教材，旨在将商务英语写作知识、技能与实际业务活动有机地结合在一起，引导学生探索商务文本的组织结构、语言特征和写作要领，培养学生的商务英语文本撰写能力和跨文化交际能力。

本书以常用商务文本为载体，设置5大学习模块：Office Administration（办公管理）、Recruitment and Employment（招聘求职）、Corporate Promotion（企业宣传）、External Corporate Communication（企业对外交流）和 Fundamentals of Business Writing（商务写作基础），全书共有20个单元，涵盖了外经贸行业从业人员必须掌握的常用商务文本。

本教材体现了"以就业为导向，以职业能力培养为核心"的人才培养理念，能够有效地提升高等职业院校学生和外经贸从业人员的商务英语写作能力。

本书封面贴有清华大学出版社防伪标签，无标签者不得销售。
版权所有，侵权必究。举报：010-62782989，beiqinquan@tup.tsinghua.edu.cn。

图书在版编目(CIP)数据

商务英语写作/房玉靖，马国志主编.—2版.—北京：清华大学出版社，2021.3（2025.1 重印）
ISBN 978-7-302-52098-6

Ⅰ.①商… Ⅱ.①房… ②马… Ⅲ.①商务—英语—写作—高等职业教育—教材 Ⅳ.①F7

中国版本图书馆CIP数据核字(2019)第009940号

责任编辑：陈立静
装帧设计：杨玉兰
责任校对：周剑云
责任印制：丛怀宇

出版发行：清华大学出版社
网　　址：https://www.tup.com.cn，https://www.wqxuetang.com
地　　址：北京清华大学学研大厦A座　　邮　　编：100084
社 总 机：010-83470000　　邮　　购：010-62786544
投稿与读者服务：010-62776969，c-service@tup.tsinghua.edu.cn
质量反馈：010-62772015，zhiliang@tup.tsinghua.edu.cn
课件下载：https://www.tup.com.cn，010-62791865

印 装 者：三河市龙大印装有限公司
经　　销：全国新华书店
开　　本：185mm×260mm　　印　　张：16.5　　字　　数：408千字
版　　次：2011年6月第1版　　2021年3月第2版
印　　次：2025年1月第7次印刷
定　　价：49.00元

产品编号：073682-01

前　言

本书是依据我国高等职业院校商务英语专业的培养目标和教学要求，结合高等职业院校学生应聘岗位的需要而编写的一部教材。本教材旨在将商务英语写作知识、技能与实际业务活动有机地结合在一起，引导学生探索商务文本的组织结构、语言特征和写作要领，培养学生的商务英语文本撰写能力和跨文化交际能力。

本教材第1版自2011年6月出版以来，众多高等职业院校师生和外经贸从业人员对其赞誉有加，同时提出了诸多宝贵的意见与建议。为了进一步完善本教材，我们实地调研了近两年涉外企事业单位对商务助理、文员的岗位能力的需求，结合高等职业院校学生的学习特点，根据任务驱动型教学需要，最终编写成本教材的第2版。

在修订过程中，我们沿用了本教材第1版的编写思路：基于岗位典型工作任务，以常用商务文本为载体，设置5大学习模块：Office Administration（办公管理）、Recruitment and Employment（招聘求职）、Corporate Promotion（企业宣传）、External Corporate Communication（企业对外交流）和 Fundamentals of Business Writing（商务写作基础），全书共有20个单元，涵盖了外经贸行业商务助理、文员必须掌握的常用商务文本。每个单元设有5个板块（19单元和20单元设有两个板块），具体如下所述。

（1）每单元开头设置了 Learning Objectives 栏目，使学生能够明确该单元的学习任务以及需要达到的知识目标和能力目标。

（2）增加了 Warm-up Case Study（热身案例研究）栏目，提供一个典型文本并加以简要分析，引导学生讨论所给文本的组织结构、语言特征和写作要领，激发学生对商务文本写作的兴趣，为接下来的文本写作训练打下基础。

前 言

（3）每单元的 Opening the Treasure Box，增补了 Related Expressions（相关表达语）和 Functional Sentences（功能句）两个栏目，便于学生在文本写作中有更多的功能语句可以借鉴，由此增强商务英语表达能力。

（4）进一步丰富了课后练习题型，有利于学生提高商务文本写作能力。

（5）更换了每单元中的部分例文，使之更具典型性，以提高学生的学习兴趣和学习效果。

（6）仔细审核并改正了本教材第 1 版中的语言表述的疏漏之处，使语言更加简洁明了，可读性更强。

为鼓励学生独立完成课后练习题，本教材课后练习题的答案将以电子书形式提供。配套的电子课件与习题答案可在清华大学出版社官网上进行下载。

本教材体现了"以就业为导向，以职业能力培养为核心"的人才培养理念，能够有效地提升高等职业院校学生和外经贸从业人员的商务英语写作能力。在教材编写过程中，我们参考了国内外诸多优秀的商务英语写作教材、翻译教材和相关网站，在此向各位作者深表谢意。

本教材由天津商务职业学院的房玉靖、马国志担任主编，鞠媛媛、王琪、董陶担任副主编。由于编者水平和时间所限，书中难免存在疏漏和错误，敬请广大读者批评指正。

编　者
2020 年 9 月

目 录

Module 1 Office Administration ······ 1

    Unit 1 Notice ······ 3

    Unit 2 Certificate ······ 15

    Unit 3 Memo ······ 28

    Unit 4 Meeting Agenda ······ 41

    Unit 5 Meeting Minutes ······ 51

    Unit 6 Business Report ······ 64

Module 2 Recruitment and Employment ······ 77

    Unit 7 Job Advertisement ······ 79

    Unit 8 Job Application Letter ······ 92

    Unit 9 Rèsumè ······ 105

    Unit 10 Letter of Recommendation ······ 117

Module 3 Corporate Promotion ······ 127

    Unit 11 Corporate Profile ······ 129

    Unit 12 Instruction ······ 144

    Unit 13 Sales Letter ······ 157

    Unit 14 Press Release ······ 170

目 录

Module 4 External Corporate Communication **187**

    Unit 15 Letter of Congratulation 189

    Unit 16 Letter of Sympathy/Condolence 199

    Unit 17 Complaints and Replies 210

    Unit 18 Business Visits and Itineraries 222

Module 5 Fundamentals of Business Writing **235**

    Unit 19 Basic Requirements for Business Writing 237

    Unit 20 Word-selecting and Sentence-making 247

Module 1

Office Administration

Notice

Part I Warm-up Case Study

Fasten your belt! You can begin an exciting journey towards learning to write a notice efficiently by reading the following sample notice. While studying the sample, you need to discuss its function, components, types and writing style. Finally, you are expected to explore the writing techniques on drafting a notice in a professional way. Now let's come to the following notice.

VICTORIA INTERNATIONAL HIGH SCHOOL
NOTICE
April.12, 2014
TREE PLANTATION DRIVE

    The Environment Club of our school is organizing a Tree Plantation Drive on Arbor Day. Under this drive 100 new trees will be planted on the campus. Tree seeds and saplings will also be distributed. All the students are invited to take part in the drive which will be inaugurated by the School Principal on April 24 at 9:00 a.m. in the school green belt.

Mary Carey
Secretary

    Have you got some ideas about how to write a notice after studying the above sample? If so, you are expected to do a brief analysis of the above sample and write down the key points.

KEY POINTS HERE

_____
_____
_____
_____
_____
_____

Part II Having a Clear Picture

I. Concept of Notices

A notice is a very short piece of writing which is usually formal in style. It is widely used by individuals and organizations to announce events and celebrations, births and deaths, occasions like inaugurations or sales, to issue public instructions, to make appeals and to extend invitations besides to issue notices of termination to the employees or the other way round i.e. notice of leaving the job from the employee to the employer.

Most notices are meant to be pinned up or pasted on special boards meant for this specific purpose only. There must be one or more such notice boards in the school and other organizations. However, notices issued by the Government departments and other big organizations also appear in various newspapers.

II. Components of Notices

A notice should give complete information and must be written in a clear and lucid style and easily understandable language. A good effective notice must include the following parts: title, body, name of the issuer and date.

1. Title

Title, also called heading, should be made very clearly. A suitable description/eye-catching heading can hold the immediate attention of the reader.

2. Body

Body is mainly about the information that is being conveyed, including details of schedule i. e. date, time, venue, program, duration, etc.

3. Name of the Issuer

It refers to the name of the person, organization, institution or office issuing the notice.

4. Date

It refers to the date of issuing included in a particular notice.

III. Types of Notices

Notices can be sent in many different ways, such as, posted up on the notice board or bulletin board, advertised on the newspaper, or sent as a letter or an e-mail. According to the ways they are released, they usually fall into four forms: form of poster, form of leaflet, form of mail and form of public signs.

1. Form of Poster

A poster is a placard displayed in a public place to announce or advertise something. Information on when and where a particular activity is going to take place will be provided in this form as the message conveyed is short and simple. A poster should be eye-catching in layout, clear in content and brief in language.

2. Form of Leaflet

A leaflet notice contains more information and is often used as a way of promotion. When writing a leaflet notice, you should make it eye-pleasing and reader-friendly.

3. Form of Mail

A notice in this form has a great popularity with people today. A mail notice may be the most efficient way to provide information to the public. It is very quick, economical and easy to send.

4. Form of Public Signs

Simplicity is most appreciated for public signs when acting as warning.

IV. Tips for Notice Writing

(1) Notices can use capital letters for details such as names of organizations, captions, and an important detail within the message itself.

(2) The date of the notice can be placed at the top right or left, or bottom right or left hand corner.

(3) Complete sentences need not always be used in all types of notices. Abbreviations and symbols can also be used.

(4) Usually future time references predominate over other tense forms.

Part III   Showing Your Talent Slightly

Now that you have had a clear picture of the components and types of notices, you can fulfill the following situational task with the help of the Warm-up Case Study.

I. Situational Task

Suppose you are the manager of the Pearl Garden, an apartment house. As the annual maintenance is arranged on Monday, Feb. 2, the power will be cut off from 7:00 a.m. to 5:00 p.m. Please write a notice to the residents. Use the mail format.

II. Do It Yourself

_____
_____
_____
_____
_____
_____
_____
_____
_____
_____

Part IV Opening the Treasure Box

I. Samples

Sample 1 A Notice about a Lecture

NOTICE

All Are Warmly Welcome

Under the auspices of the Teaching Affairs Section

A report will be given on

Contemporary American Economy

By

Visiting American Prof. Smith

In

The Reading Room of the Library

On Tuesday, May 14, 2018, at 2:00 p.m.

May 10, 2018

Sample 2 A Notice about a New Position

NOTICE

It is hereby announced that upon the decision of the board of directors Miss Sophia White is appointed Personnel Manager.

The Managing Director's Office

Jan. 10, 2018

Sample 3 A Notice about a Missing Girl

A GIRL MISSING

My pretty girl, named Sally Su, aged 4, in red blouse, got lost on yesterday morning of April 21, 2014, when we went shopping in Carrefour Supermarket. She is 1.10 meters tall, with black hair, round face, rosy cheeks, big eyes, and a small mole on chin. She can speak daily Chinese, not very fluently.

Whoever meets her or knows her whereabouts or has any information about her location is begged to advise her family or ring them up.

A thousand thanks from Tom Wang and his family.

Add: 125 Zhujiang Road, Hexi District, Tianjin
Tel: 13012349606

Sample 4 A Notice about a Lost Check

CHECK LOST

July 15, 2018

Lost, one check No. 98563 for the sum of $123,000 drawn on the Agriculture Bank, Xinjiang Branch, dated July 14, 2018. Payment has been stopped and check declared null and void.

Good Fortune Company

Sample 5 A Removal Notice

REMOVAL NOTICE

Banca Commercial Italian

Tianjin Representative Office

Please be informed that as from March 10, 2018

our new address is as follows:

6 Xinhua Road, Hepei District, Tianjin

Tel: 23564879

Fax: 23564880

Sample 6 A Notice about a Conference

Annual General Meeting of Shareholders

Notice is hereby given that Goldsphere Holding Limited will hold the third Annual General Meeting of its shareholders at the Tianjin Hotel, Jade Hall, on Monday December 16, 2014, at 6:00 p. m. for the following purposes:

(1) To receive and consider the Company's Accounts and the Reports of the Directors and Auditors for the year ended September 30, 2014.

(2) To declare a final dividend.

(3) To elect Directors.

(4) To appoint Auditors and fix their remunerations.

(5) To transact any other business.

Lam Smith

Secretary

November 20, 2014

Sample 7 A Notice about the Delay of Examination

Dear Examinees,

As you know, due to unfortunate circumstances, ETS was forced to cancel the scores of the October 2014 TOEFL administration in the People's Republic of China. At that time, you were notified that you would be able to take another TOEFL without charge up through the October 2015 administration. You should be aware that the TOEFL program has a long standing policy of not refunding test fees when administrations are cancelled.

We apologize for any inconvenience that this may cause to you.

Russell Webster

(Signature)

Executive Director

TOEFL Program

Educational Testing Service

Sample 8 A Notice about the Opening of New Business

Dear Sirs,

We would like to bring to your notice the fact that we have established ourselves as a trading firm under this name and address:

Huaxin Trading Co., Ltd.

130 Nanjing Road, Tianjin, PRC

For more than 15 years we have been the Tianjin representatives for U.S.A. Trading Co., Ltd. We can offer you an unusually large variety of first-class electric machines at strictly competitive prices.

We look forward to establishing business relationship with you.

Yours faithfully,

Carl Yang

Sample 9 A Notice about a New Product

Dear Mr. Smith,

I am proud of announcing that Homeland's has just signed a contract with Ponnin Paint Company, giving us exclusive distribution of the Ponnin line in North China.

For years we have experienced tough going in paint and varnish sales because we were competing with Ponnin products. Now it's a different story. Why compete when there's a better way? This is indeed a happy occasion for us!

I've enclosed a color brochure, "Meet Ponnin—the World's Best Paint." Please read it carefully, for it tells the story of Ponnin's success much better than I could.

> I am also enclosing an order blank for your convenience. Don't forget, your credit is unlimited at Homeland's, and we invite you to try out some of the Ponnin brands. You won't be sorry!
>
> Sincerely,
> Ma Ning

II. Related Expressions

(1) mole   *n.*   色素　痣

(2) remuneration   *n.* 报酬

Our company offers a competitive remuneration package, including a company car.
本公司提供一套具有竞争力的报酬组合，包括一辆公司分派的汽车。

(3) Please be informed that...   请知悉，兹告知

Please be informed that from now on our telephone number will change to 23564879.
请知悉从现在起我们的电话号码改为 23564879。

(4) due to   由于……

Due to the recent government financial cuts, we have been forced to make the following changes.
由于最近政府削减财政，我们不得不作出以下调整。

(5) under the auspices of   在……的资助（赞助）下

a relief project set up under the auspices of the United Nations
由联合国资助的救济项目

(6) It is hereby announced that...   现予公告……

It is hereby announced that Professor Lee Guang has been elected deputy to the conference.
李光教授当选为大会代表，现予公告。

(7) appoint sb. as sth.   任命某人……

The School Board have appointed her Superintendent of the city's schools.
学校董事会任命她为该市所有学校的督学。

(8) beg sb. to do sth.   恳求某人做某事

The children begged to come with us.
孩子们恳求和我们一起来。

(9) null and void   （法律）无效的

The contract was declared null and void.

该合同被宣布无效。

(10) Notice is hereby given that...　兹声明……

Notice is hereby given on behalf of Joint Venture BNC Co.

兹代表中外合资精豪时装厂声明。

(11) please find enclosed...　兹附上……

Please find enclosed an agenda for the meeting.

兹附上会议议程表。

(12) Details of the quiz are as follows:

以下是知识竞赛的具体要求：

(13) I am writing to announce my resignation from... , effective two weeks from this date.

我宣布从……辞职，并于两周后正式离职。

(14) The notice covers these points:

本通告包含以下几点内容：

(15) If you have any questions about how the Plan works or your rights and obligations under the Plan, please contact the Plan Administrator at...

如果您有关于此方案的任何问题或是想了解方案中你方的权利与义务，请通过以下方式与我们的方案负责人联系。

III. Functional Sentences

(1) We enclose our list of prices and terms, and would ask you to kindly note the signatures at foot.

兹附上价目表及交易条款，并请注意下面的签名。

(2) It is proclaimed that the board of directors has decided to dismiss Mr. John Smith from the post of chief of the president's office.

校董事会决定免去约翰·史密斯先生校长办公室主任的职务。

(3) I inform you that I have now removed my factory to the above address.

本厂已迁移到上述地址，特此通知。

(4) Having established ourselves in this city, as merchants and general agents, we take the liberty of acquainting you of it, and solicit the preference of your order.

我方已在本市开设贸易与总代理店，特此通知。同时，恳请订购。

(5) By this we inform you that we have today paid Mr. Smith $100.

今天我们已付给史密斯先生100美元，特此告知。

(6) We declare all these documents invalid.

现声明这些文件均已作废。

(7) We are pleased to inform you that our business will be turned into a limited company

on the May 1.

本公司将于5月1日改为股份有限公司,特此奉告。

(8) Notice is hereby given that annual general meeting of the shareholders of our company will be held at the Bankers Club on March 1.

本公司股东年会,将于3月1日在银行家俱乐部召开,特此函告。

(9) Authorized by Li Wei, Chairman of the Board of Directors of China Xinhua Industries Group, I declare the following.

由中国新华工业集团董事长李伟先生授权声明如下。

(10) The visit to Friendship Hospital, originally scheduled for tomorrow is now put off until further notice.

原定于明天参观友谊医院,现在取消,具体时间另行通知。

(11) All individuals are hereby informed that a legislation regarding "Ban of Smoking in Public" has been approved.

公共场所禁烟条例已颁布,特此公告。

(12) Starting from July 20, the law will come into effect.

本法律自7月20日起生效。

(13) Please accept my notice of resignation from Star Trading Company, effective April 23, 2014.

本人决定从星光贸易公司辞职,于2014年4月23日离职,特此通告。

(14) I hope a two-week notice provides you ample time to find a replacement for my post.

我希望提前两周的离职通知可以给公司足够的时间去招聘到本岗位的新人。

(15) All citizens are requested to donate blood for noble cause.

希望全体公民都能够积极参与无偿献血活动。

(16) This is to notify that the school is organizing "Annual General Knowledge Quiz" on May 14, Friday, at 2:00 p. m.

学校计划于5月14日,周五下午2点举行"年度常识问答竞赛",特此通知。

(17) For any clarification or enquiry, contact Miss Agness, personally or at this number 92339333.

不明事宜请联系艾格尼斯小姐或致电92339333。

(18) If I can be of any help during the transition, please don't hesitate to ask.

在过渡期间,我愿意为公司提供任何帮助。

(19) Please accept this as my formal notice of resignation from XYZ Company.

我正式宣布从XYZ公司辞职,特此通告。

(20) All the students are invited to take part in the drive.

特邀请全体学生参加本次活动。

Part V Displaying Your Prowess Fully

I. You will read a notice on HUKO New Year party. It is in a mail format. Can you make it in a poster format?

December 25, 2014
HUKO NEW YEAR PARTY

Dear all staff of HUKO,

We wish to invite you to the HUKO NEW YEAR PARTY at Multi-functional Hall in Staff House starting at 7:30 p. m. on Saturday, December 28, 2014.

You may bring two friends to the party. Please bring a small gift (suggested price HK$20) to be swapped among others.

See you at the party.

Staff Relations

II. Please write a notice according to the hints given below.

请为教育学院写一则招租启事，每年暑假七、八月份都有来自国外的学生到教育学院进行短期的课程学习，但学院不能提供足够的宿舍，希望有意为访问学生（年龄14岁到18岁）提供住宿的居民与王明先生联系。

III. Please write a notice according to the hints given.

通 告

CMK 长海进出口有限公司和里通运输有限公司的代理协议已于 2014 年 4 月 30 日终止。自 2014 年 5 月 1 日起，里通公司不再承担 CMK 公司的商业活动和代理经销等职责。特此通告。

里通运输有限公司
2014 年 4 月 30 日

IV. The following notice is not well done. Please revise it.

Dear residents,

We will close the Staff House Office during Chinese New Year holidays and we will open it again on Feb. 4, 2014.

Only a few staff will be on duty during the holidays; thus, we cannot offer the room cleaning services. We will resume it on Feb. 4, 2014 also.

If there is any emergency, you can call our duty staff at the Service Counter at 22491806 or 98016620 for assistance.

Regards,

Rocky Tang (Mr.)
Manager

V. Please write a notice according to the Chinese giren below.

2014年8月14日刊登在《中国日报》第五版的 CCQSEM 广告，应作如下更正。华星技术检验有限公司应为华锌技术检验有限公司，公司电话号码应为 8429908 和 83166688 转 835。

Certificate

Part I Warm-up Case Study

Fasten your belt! You can begin an exciting journey towards learning to write a certificate efficiently by reading the following sample certificates. While studying the samples, you need to discuss their function, components, types and writing style. Finally, you are expected to explore the writing techniques on drafting a certificate in a professional way. Now let's come to the following certificates.

Case 1

Certificate of Achievement

This certificate is awarded to

John Smith

In recognition of outstanding performance in Leadership

Orientation Training Program

Signature   **Date**

Case 2

Salary Certificate

    This is to certify that Mr./Miss/Mrs._____ (Name of Employee) is working with our esteemed organization/company under the title of _____ (Title of Employee) since _____ (Date of inception of job). We found he/she fully committed to his/her job and totally sincere toward this organization/company.

    We are issuing this letter on the specific request of our employee without accepting any liability on behalf of this letter or part of this letter on our organization/company.

Regards,
[Company Signature]
[Company stamped]
[Date]

    Have you got some ideas about how to write a certificate after studying the above samples? If so, you are expected to do a brief analysis of the above samples and write down the key points.

KEY POINTS HERE

_____
_____
_____
_____
_____
_____
_____
_____
_____

Part II Having a Clear Picture

I. Concept of Certificates

Certificates are official documents stating that a particular fact is true, providing who one is or showing one's ability, degree, experience or status, etc. Certificates are issued by organizations in authority as proof or evidence of something.

II. Components of Certificates

There are some common elements in a certificate.

1. Title

It is the heading at the top of a certificate, which tells the type of the certificate. It's common to set the title in a larger size, perhaps even in a different color from the rest of the text.

2. Presentation Wording

Following the title, it is customary to include one of these phrases or a variation:

- is awarded to
- is hereby awarded to
- is presented to
- is given to
- is hereby bestowed upon

Additionally, even though the title of the award may say Certificate of Appreciation, the following line may start out with "This certificate is presented to" or similar wording.

3. Recipient's Name

It is common to have the name of the recipient emphasized in some way. The name of the recipient (shown in italics) may also appear in a larger or decorative font.

4. Description

A descriptive paragraph that gives more specifics of why a person or group is receiving the certificate is optional. In the case of a Perfect Attendance Award the title is self-explanatory. For other types of certificates, especially when several are being presented for different accomplishments, it is customary to describe the reason that an individual is getting the recognition. This descriptive text may start out with such phrases as:

- in recognition of
- in appreciation for
- for achievements in
- for outstanding achievements in

5. Date

Formats for dates on a certificate can take many forms. The date can come before or after the description of the reason for the award. The date is typically the date on which the award is made while the specific dates for which the award applies may be set out in the title or descriptive text. Some examples:

- is presented on October 31, 2014
- is awarded on the 31st of October, 2014
- on this 31st day of October

6. Signature

Signatures can make a certificate seem more real, more legitimate. If you know ahead of time who will be signing the certificate you can add their printed name beneath the signature line.

III. Types of Certificates

(1) A document establishing the authenticity of certain details of an item, event, or transaction: a certificate of birth.

(2) A document issued to a person completing a course of study not leading to a diploma.

(3) A document certifying that a person may officially practice in certain professions.

(4) A document certifying ownership.

IV. Tips for Certificate Writing

(1) Formality and conciseness are required in writing a certificate.

(2) A proper format is preferred when a certificate is drafted.

(3) It is guaranteed that the information from the certificate is true and correct.

Part III Showing Your Talent Slightly

Now that you have had a clear picture of the components and types of certificates, you can fulfill the following situational task with the help of the Warm-up Case Study.

I. Situational Task

You work as an office clerk in President's Office, Tianhai Co., Ltd. This morning, Miss Huang, the Office Chief asks you to issue a certificate of employment for Mr. Li Wei, a former employee in the company. The information is given below.

李伟，男，1980年8月12日生，自2010年7月至2014年7月，在我公司（天海公司）担任进出口部经理职务。任职期间，勤勉努力并在履行职责方面显示出才能和智慧，获得同事和上司的敬重。李伟离职，系出于自愿。

II. Do It Yourself

Certificate

August 1, 2014

To whom it may concern,

_____

_____

_____

_____

_____(official stamp)

Tianhai Co., Ltd.

Part IV Opening the Treasure Box

I. Samples

Sample 1

[Write the name of the university here]
This certifies that

[Name & Other information]

has successfully completed the required course of study approved by
the Board of Education for the state of [State], and is therefore awarded
this

Degree

Given this _____ day of _____ 2014

_____   _____
       Superintendent   Principal

Sample 2

Sample 3

Sample 4

Sample 5

Sample 6

Pamela O. Feliciano
3831 Harter Street
Dayton, OH 45407

Dear Ms. Feliciano,

We are writing this letter to certify the qualifications of Chad S. Deloach in regards to his post secondary education at Clear Water Creek Community College.

During the period of 2010—2014, Chad attended classes at our institution. He studied in the areas of business management, accounting and economics. He completed the required course load in all these areas. He completed his co-op requirement in the summer of 2006, and wrote all the necessary exams.

Throughout all his studies, he achieved a 3.8 GPA, one of the highest in his class. He won the respect of all his teachers and peers through his hard work and dedication to his studies. He has shown himself to be an upstanding citizen, and would be a great asset to your organization.

Sincerely,

Krista R. Kish

Sample 7

To whom it may concern,

This letter is to certify that Miss Eleanor Crumhorn is employed at J.O.B Logistics, currently working on the Fulsome Fashion Warehouse project.

At this time she is our lead coordinator and is responsible for developing the day-to-day system that will soon be implemented for their online shipping requirements.

I have issued this certification by request of Miss Eleanor Crumhorn, and it may be used for whatever purpose she sees fit.

Regards,
Signed
Mr. D. Crowe
Human Resources

Sample 8

To whomever it may concern,

I am writing to certify that Mr. Samuel Kitchen completed a 6-week term of work experience at Mr. Chips Computing, as a shop floor sales assistant, from Jan. 1, 2012 to Dec. 30, 2012.

During his time here we found him to be satisfactory in terms of communication skills, but he showed particular knowledge in personal computing, which we feel over time would help him to develop into a model employee.

We wish him all the best in his future career choices.

Signed
Mr. Holloway
Manager of Mr. Chips Computing

Sample 9

Sara L. Brown
3146 Holden Street
Metropolis, IL 62960

This letter is to certify that James Brown worked as a general accountant at Triangle Corp. for the period from November 5, 2010 to December 12, 2014.

While at our company, his responsibilities were to design and implement pricing controls in relation to our line of mathematical measuring devices.

Through our working relationship, I came to appreciate the attention to detail that James showed for his work and was deeply saddened when he departed our company. I know that he will do a great job wherever you put him in your organization.

Sincerely,
Joseph Mancini

II. Related Expressions

(1) This is to certify that...　兹证明……

(2) To whom it may concern　敬启者

(3) be employed in our sales department as a sales manager
　　在销售部担任销售经理一职

(4) be enrolled to study in the accounting department of Tianjin University
　　被天津大学会计系录取

(5) It is advised that...　建议……

(6) I have the pleasure to give evidence that...　我非常高兴地向您证明……

(7) display his ability in cooperation and leadership
　　表现出了他很强的合作能力和领导能力

(8) be promoted to vice president　被提升为副总裁

(9) be engaged in import and export business　从事进出口业务

(10) be hereby awarded　授予……

(11) bear all his expenses　为他担负所有费用

(12) be qualified to work as...　胜任……工作

(13) complete all the courses and pass all the examinations　修业期满，成绩合格

(14) For outstanding service to...　对……作出杰出贡献

(15) In recognition of commitment to a standard of excellence　优秀典范，特此表彰

III. Functional Sentences

(1) This certifies that Miss Zheng Fang has been employed in our public relations department for five years.
　　兹证明，郑芳小姐在我公司公关部工作已有 5 年。

(2) At college, he was an excellent student; in the company, he is an outstanding engineer.
　　他在学校是一名优秀的学生，在公司是一位杰出的工程师。

(3) I have the pleasure to give evidence that Miss Chang Fengyan is qualified to work as an electronics engineer in your company.
　　我非常高兴地向您证明常凤艳小姐能够胜任贵公司电子工程师的职位。

(4) He is a very able man with a strong sense of responsibility and great enthusiasm for helping others.
　　他能力很强，有责任感，乐于助人。

(5) Mr. Zhang Bao is now leaving our company as we have no further need of his service.

因为我公司压缩人员编制，张宝先生离职。

(6) Mr. Sun Feng has been selected to take a refresher course at Cambridge University.

孙峰先生被选派到剑桥大学进修。

(7) It is suggested that he needs a rest for fifteen days, and if necessary, comes back for a check by that time.

他被建议休息15天，15天后复查。

(8) She was enrolled in September, 2014 to study in the Business Administration Department of Xiangjiang University as a postgraduate in Business English.

她于2014年9月被香江大学商务管理系录取为商务英语专业研究生。

(9) In accordance with academic rules of the People's Republic of China, the master's degree of Engineering is hereby awarded.

符合中华人民共和国学位管理规定，授予工程硕士学位。

(10) The patent right of the Trademark Registration belongs to Tiancheng Compang. Attached below is the Pictorial Trademark.

该商标的专利权属于天成公司，商标图案附后。

(11) This is to certify that Mr. Yang Lei has won the title of Rising Star for his outstanding work.

杨磊先生工作出色，被授予新星奖。

(12) He is in good health and capable of working eight hours a day.

他身体健康，能够胜任每天8小时的工作。

(13) Mr. Zhang Wei has never been sanctioned legally during his inhabitation in the People's Republic of China.

张伟先生在中国居住期间没有刑事犯罪记录。

(14) During the time he faithfully attended to his duties.

在职期间，他认真履职，恪尽职守。

(15) He completed the required course load in all these areas.

他完成了本专业全部课程的学习。

(16) I have issued this certification by request of Miss Eleanor Crumhorn, and it may be used for whatever purpose she sees fit.

应埃莉诺·克鲁姆小姐的请求，我特出具此证明。

(17) I know that he will do a great job wherever you put him in your organization.

我相信他可以胜任贵公司任何一个职位。

(18) If you have any further queries about this matter, please feel free to contact us.

如有任何问题，请及时与我们联系。

(19) I am writing to officially certify that I, Ursula Glenister, currently reside at 635

Benjamin Hill, Austin, Texas 88114, and have been present at this address for 10 years, since February 3, 2001.

本人乌苏拉·格兰斯特现居住在德克萨斯州奥斯丁市本杰明希尔路635号，邮编88114，本人从2001年2月3日起即在此居住，至今已经10年，特此证明。

(20) I certify that Mr. Langston Manuel, has a stake of 30 percent ownership in Lion Energy, Licence #UIOUYT67T6, and also a stake of 10 percent ownership in Olivia Electricity, Licence #HSTY7654IKH.

兰斯顿·曼纽尔先生持有莱恩能源公司30%的股份，编号为#UIOUYT67T6，同时拥有奥利维亚电力公司10%的股份，编号为#HSTY7654IKH，特此证明。

Part V Displaying Your Prowess Fully

I. Draft a certificate of achievement for postgraduate training program according to the hints given below.

赵晓梅，女，生于1992年7月5日，于2010年9月至2014年6月在九江学院英语语言文学专业研究生课程班学习，按研究生培养计划已完成全部课程，修业期满，考试成绩合格，已达到硕士研究生同等学历水平，特发此证。

II. Draft a certificate of retirement according to the hints given below.

钱敏，女，55岁，符合国家退休规定，2014年5月1日从锦江医院退休。

III. Fill in the blanks to complete the following identity certificate.

```
Identity Certificate
```

_____(1)_____（兹证明）that Dr. Green, an American citizen, male, aged 45, is a professor of English in the employ of our school. He _____(2)_____（持有美国护照）and lives in Room 525, the Foreign Guest House of our school. Dr. Green _____(3)_____（申报了临时户口）with the Foreign Affairs Department of Songjiang Security Bureau.

（Signature）
Foreign Affairs Office
Lantian University

IV. Draft a letter of appointment according to the hints given below.

聘请周虹小姐为前景公司法律顾问。聘期自2010年1月至2012年1月。

V. Draft a notarial certificate for trademark registration according to the hints given below.

中国天成公司生产的晶体管收音机的红梅商标注册证（编号为 1086 号）系中国工商行政管理总局出具。该商标的专利权属于中国天成公司，商标图案附后。中华人民共和国上海市公证处在 2014 年 10 月 5 日出具该公证书。

VI. Fill in the blanks to complete the following certificate.

Marriage Certificate

Serial No. 269568

May 1, 2014

Liu Hong and Zhang Ling _____(1)_____ (自愿结婚). _____(2)_____ (经审核), it is found _____(3)_____ (符合结婚的规定) of the Marriage Law of the People's Republic of China. They are given this marriage certificate.

（Seal）

Marriage Registration Office

Tianjin Bureau of Civil Affairs

Memo

Part I Warm-up Case Study

Fasten your belt! You can begin an exciting journey towards learning to write a memo efficiently by reading the following sample memo. While studying the sample, you need to discuss its function, components, types and writing style. Finally, you are expected to explore the writing techniques on drafting a memo in a professional way. Now let's come to the following memo.

Memo to Coworkers

TO: All Staff and Interns
FROM: Ana Lucily, Executive Assistant to the President
DATE: July 15, 2012
SUBJECT: Dishes in the Sink

It has come to our attention that there has been a pile of unwashed dishes that accumulates in the sink by the end of each week. It has gotten so bad that washing one's hands in the kitchen sink becomes an uncomfortable undertaking. Therefore, we are introducing a new policy that mandates that employees wash their dishes as soon as they are done with them, keeping the sink clear for other uses.

If you do not have the time to wash your lunch container or coffee mug, leave it by your desk until you are ready to wash it. Even two or three dirty plates will encourage every person thereafter to leave their unwashed, food-stained dishes and silverware in the sink. Conversely, studies have shown that when a sink is empty, people are more likely to wash their dishes immediately.

Thank you for your cooperation!

Best,
Ana Lucily

Have you got some ideas about how to write a memo after studying the above sample? If so, you are expected to do a brief analysis of the above sample and write down the key points.

KEY POINTS HERE

_____

Part II　Having a Clear Picture

I. Concept of Memos

A memo is short for the Latin word memorandum. A memorandum is a letter, in a sense, and can be either formal or informal. It is a common form of communication in the workplace. It provides an easy way to convey information or ideas to your coworkers or employees in a quick and informative way. Interoffice memos are frequently used to announce staff meetings, employee promotions, vacation schedules, and so on; issue instructions; transmit other documents; provide information in the form of informal reports; summarize and confirm the results of departmental meetings and the major points of discussions among staff.

II. Components of Memos

The format of a memo varies from company to company. However, all memos, regardless of format, include a heading and a body.

1. Heading

The heading of a memo always includes the name and the job title of the recipient, the name and the job title of the sender, the date, and the subject line. Make the subject line as specific as possible. The layout of the heading is like the following.

Memo

TO: the name and the job title of the recipient

FROM: the name and the job title of the sender

DATE: the complete date when the memo is written

SUBJECT: what the memo is about

2. Body

(1) A memo does not begin with a salutation like "Dear Mr. Edwards". Instead, dive right into your opening segment that introduces the matter you're discussing in the memo.

(2) Introduce the problem or issue in the first paragraph. Briefly give the recipients the context behind the action you wish them to take. This is somewhat like a thesis statement, which introduces the topic and states why it matters. You might also consider the introduction as an abstract, or a summary of the entire memo.

(3) Give context for the issue at hand. Your readers may need some background information about the issue you're addressing. Give some context, but be brief and only state what is necessary.

(4) Support your course of action in the discussion segment. Give a short summary of the actions that will be implemented. Give evidence and logical reasons for the solutions you propose. Start with the most important information, and then move to specific or supporting facts. State how the readers will benefit from taking the action you recommend, or be disadvantaged through lack of action.

(5) Suggest the actions that the readers should take. A memo is a call for action on a particular issue, whether it is an announcement about a new company product, new policies regarding expense reports, or a statement about how the company is addressing a problem. Restate the action that the readers should take in the closing paragraph or sentence.

(6) Close the memo with a positive and warm summary. The memo's final paragraph should restate the next steps to address the issue at hand. It should also include a warm note that reiterates the solidarity of the organization.

III. Types of Memos

Memos can be typed according to their circulation way. Generally speaking, there are four types of memos.

(1) To upper management. This kind of memo is acting as a report and goes to upper management.

(2) To divisions affiliated. This type of memo usually carries instructions from upper management.

(3) To all the staff. This sort of memo works as a notice or bulletin.

(4) To colleagues in or outside one's own department. This kind of memo can be regarded as information exchanging.

IV. Tips for Memo Writing

(1) Organize your thoughts before writing a memo.

(2) Master the format of a basic memo.

(3) Simplify your information.

(4) Put numbers before each matter so that the message can be understood clearly.

(5) Set a space line between each paragraph so that your reader can make better sense about the idea carried in the memo.

(6) Check your spelling, grammar and punctuation before sending out your memo.

Part III Showing Your Talent Slightly

Now that you have had a clear picture of the components and types of memos, you can fulfill the following situational task with the help of the Warm-up Case Study.

I. Situational Task

Instructions: Read the question carefully. Working in pairs, draft a memo that would best present the following information.

Scenario: In recent months, your company staff has not been punctual in reporting for work. Your general manager has taken note of the worrying trend and asked you, the HR executive to nip the problem in the bud.

Task: Write a memo to your company staff. Ensure that your message is clear, concise, courteous and complete. Include in your memo:

(1) The importance of being punctual.

(2) Some recommendations on how they can be punctual.

Top 5 reasons for being late:

- Could not get a taxi.

- MRT train broke down.
- Overslept.
- Got caught in the traffic jam.
- Heavy rain.

II. Do It Yourself

Memo

To:

From:

Date:

Subject:

_____

_____

_____

Part IV   Opening the Treasure Box

I. Samples

Sample 1 A Memo to Boss

To: Joe Campos, VP of Sales
From: Kate Chaplain, Senior Sales Associate
Date: April 5, 2014
Subject: Quarterly Review

Mr. Campos,

I've attached my quarterly review report to this email, but I also wanted to quickly discuss the trends I've noticed in our sales data over the past few months.

We've sold over 10,000 new memberships over the past quarter, which is a 22% increase from Q4 of last year. Our data analysis shows that this upswing corresponds with the creation of company pages on various social media sites, including Facebook and Twitter, which allows more people to connect with us virtually. In fact, over half of our new memberships were purchased from links that were posted on our Facebook and Twitter profiles.

We've also had an 82% renewal rate in memberships that were set to expire in Q1. This is 16% higher than our renewal rate in Q4, which suggests that our new program — having sales associates contact members directly about renewing their memberships — is working even better than we had expected.

Unfortunately, we haven't seen the same rapid growth in the purchase of family memberships.

While the number of FMs has increased by 2% over last quarter's numbers, I believe we can get that number even higher. I've listed some suggestions in my report, but I would also like to add it to the agenda for our quarterly review meeting later this week.

Please let me know if you have any questions.

Best Regards,
Kate Chaplain

Sample 2 A Memo for Reduction in Work Force

MEMO OF REDUCING STAFF

To: James Madison, Director
From: Philips Kingsley
Date: July 20, 2014
Subject: Reducing Staff

I have several proposals for cutting down on office staff.

First, I suggest that we eliminate the full-time position of order clerk, since there is not enough work to occupy him throughout the month. Orders and requests for sales information are heaviest at the end of the month; in contrast, there is little to do for the first two weeks of each month. Therefore, I recommend that we hire temporary help for the last two weeks of each month and give the orders from the first of the month to the sales department to process.

Second, now that our systems are completely computerized we no longer need a computer programmer on staff. It's true we will need computer programming services occasionally in the future, for instance, when we revise our billing system. In such cases, however, we can hire a freelance programmer.

Third, I suggest that I share my secretary with the assistant office manager, thus eliminating one secretarial position. Although this will increase the managerial workload, I feel we can handle it. Moreover, we can always hire temporary help to get us through particularly busy periods.

If these suggestions are followed, we should be able to save approximately $26,000 in the coming year in salaries alone. So, I believe these changes will result in greater work efficiency.

Sample 3 Employee Request to Attend a Convention

Memo

To: Adam C. Zhang

From: Helen Hunter, Training Manager

Date: February 20, 2014

Subject: ASTD Convention in New York

May I have your permission to attend the national convention of the ASTD (American Society of Training Directors) in New York from March 12 to March 15?

This year's theme is "The Electronic Classroom". There will be various presentations on the uses of the computer and other electronic equipment. Of particular interest to me is the panel "The Usage of Multimedia in Training". Equally fascinating will be forty exhibits featuring hardware and software supplied by most of the leading electronics distributors.

I estimate that my expenses would amount to $500, for travel, hotel, meals, etc. I think it will be worth that amount if we can get a deeper insight into the applications of electronics to our training program.

Sample 4 Interoffice Memo

INTEROFFICE MEMO

To: Ms. Ellen Ferraro

From: Mr. Mason, General Manager

Date: June 18, 2014

Subject: Position of Assistant Manager

As you know, our company's sales are growing rapidly these days. We will hire several new employees soon and need someone to train them. This person will also help me to manage the office staff.

I would like you to become our new assistant manager. You will be responsible for training the new employees. You will have your own secretary and a new office.

I want you to begin your duties in about 4 weeks. I am certain that you will enjoy your new responsibilities. Please talk to me soon about the arrangements.

Sample 5 A Memo Sent to Division Affiliated

Memo

To: All Departments' Managers

From: J. Geoff, Personnel Director

Date: March 5, 2014

Subject: An Advanced Part-time Deutsch Course

An advanced part-time Deutsch course is starting on the April 2, from 7:00 p.m. to 8:30 p.m. every weekday's evening (Friday is included), and finishing on the April 20. Textbooks are free but only those who can pass the test held on the March 28 are eligible to attend the course.

Please collect the names of the staff in your division who want to take the course and send the list to Mrs. Hope, the assistant of Personnel Manager, by 4:00 p.m. Thursday (March 22).

Sample 6 Interoffice Memo

INTEROFFICE MEMO

To: All Department Heads

From: Patricia Washington, General Manager

Date: April 20, 2014

Subject: Visit of German Agent

(1) Please note that Katy Schmidt, our German agent, will be visiting our company on Friday, April 20.

(2) There will be a meeting on that day at 11:30 a.m. in the boardroom, which you should all attend.

(3) Ms. Schmidt will be presenting her marketing plan for expanding sales in the German market.

(4) If you wish to join us for lunch at a local restaurant, please let me know as soon as possible.

Sample 7 Memo for Information

Memo

To: All Employees

From: Chang Jiang, Office Manager

Date: August 5, 2014

Subject: Postponement of the Weekend Outing

Because many of you have expressed a strong desire in watching the Opening Ceremony of the Olympic Games, the planned weekend outing will be postponed until a later time. Once the planning committee has set a new date, you will be informed by memo of the time, location, and date.

Thank you for your understanding.

Sample 8 Memo for Information

Memo

To: Mr. Brown

From: Joe

Date: June 26, 2014

Subject: Feedback of the New System

The Training Dept. is collecting the feedback of the operation of the new system. Please send them the report on:

(1) How long the system has been working in your Dept.

(2) What jobs it is used for.

(3) How it is working.

The report is expected by 4:00 p.m. this Friday (June 30).

II. Related Expressions

(1) memo   *n.* 备忘录

(2) eliminate   *v.* 消除，根除

(3) order   *n.* 订货，订购

(4) recommend   *v.* 劝告，建议

(5) temporary   *adj.* 暂时的，临时的

(6) revise   *v.* 改变（意见、计划等），修正

(7) workload   *n.* （人或机器的）工作量，工作负荷

(8) approximately   *adv.* 大约

(9) convention   *n.* 大会，会议

(10) application   *n.* 用途，实际应用

(11) division   *n.* （机构、公司等的）部，部门

(12) feedback   *n.* 反馈意见

(13) as instructed   依照指示

　　We returned the questionnaire as instructed.   我们依照指示交回调查表。

(14) in contrast   相比之下

　　Their old house had been large and spacious; in contrast, the new London flat seemed cramped and dark.

　　他们的老房子又大又宽敞，相比之下，伦敦的那套新公寓又窄又暗。

(15) insight into （尤指对复杂事情的）顿悟，猛省
    The article gives us a real insight into the cause of the present economic crisis.
    这篇文章分析目前经济危机的原因，发人深省。

(16) be informed by memo   以备忘录的形式通知某人

(17) Please talk to me as soon as possible.   请尽快与我联系。

(18) Please collect...   请收集……资料

(19) Studies have shown that...   研究显示……

(20) It has come to our attention that...   我们注意到……

III. Functional Sentences

(1) I hope that you will pay attention to this problem and solve it as soon as possible.
    我希望这个问题能引起你们的注意并能得到尽快地解决。

(2) The board of directors approved your proposal at the meeting last week.
    董事会在上周的会议上通过了你的建议。

(3) We have submitted this proposal to the management.
    我们已经将这个建议呈交给了管理层。

(4) Please show him around our company.
    请带他参观我们的公司。

(5) If possible, I would like to receive your report before the next board meeting.
    如果可能的话，我想在下次董事会议前收到你的报告。

(6) I have dealt with the inquiry that you passed to me on Friday.
    我已经解决了你周五提出的问题。

(7) I would like to know exactly what action has been taken.
    我想知道具体采取了什么措施。

(8) We suggest that the price should be decreased in accordance with the present marketing situation.
    依据目前的市场状况，我们建议把价格降低。

(9) Could you arrange a meeting with all the directors?
    你能否安排一次全体董事会？

(10) Can you provide us with your views on how to deal with the matter?
    你能否提供你对解决此事的看法？

(11) Please fax this information directly to me by 4: 00 p.m. on Thursday January 11.
    请于1月11日周四下午4点前将这些资料直接传真给我。

(12) I have several proposals for cutting down the cost.
    关于降低成本我有几条建议。

(13) Please feel free to contact me if you need further information.
   如需了解更多信息，请与我联系。

(14) Please let me know your response to these suggestions.
   我想知道你对于这些建议的看法。

(15) We would appreciate hearing from you in regard to this matter.
   盼望您对此事的回复。

(16) As of July 1, 2015, XYZ Corporation will be implementing new policies regarding health coverage.
   XYZ 公司自 2015 年 7 月 1 日起将实行新的员工医疗保险制度。

(17) All employees must use the new accounting system by June 1, 2015.
   自 2015 年 6 月 1 日起，全体员工需使用新的会计系统。

(18) I will be glad to discuss these recommendations with you later on and follow through on any decisions you make.
   我很愿意与您进一步讨论这些建议，并会遵从您所做出的任何决定。

(19) I've attached my quarterly review report to this email, but I also wanted to quickly discuss the trends I've noticed in our sales data over the past few months.
   随信已附上了季度报告，但我还是想在此向您简单汇报一下过去几个月公司的销售情况及发展趋势。

(20) It has come to our attention that there has been a pile of unwashed dishes that accumulates in the sink by the end of each week.
   我们注意到每周末的时候，水槽里面都堆积了很多没有清洗的餐具。

Part V Displaying Your Prowess Fully

I. Write an interoffice memo according to the hints given below.

员工孙明，由于母亲生病，无法完成原定计划的工作，需要以书面形式向上级主管请假。在这一备忘录中，孙明对自己离岗期间的工作做出了适当的安排，推荐其他人接替自己的工作。

II. Please write a memo according to the hints given below.

李卫东先生是大众办公家具公司销售部经理。写一封备忘录给张媛媛女士，内容为威海设计有限公司的总裁伊恩·马克斯先生将于 2019 年 3 月 12 日来公司参观，同时会购买一定数量的桌椅、文件柜和电脑桌。要求张媛媛女士做好准备，在洽谈会上对产品进行介绍，建议她向买方陈列本公司最好的家具样品，并准备好有关这些家具价格的资料。李卫东在备忘录中还提到，李梅以前做过类似的工作，她正好有空可以帮她。

III. Write a memo according to the hints given below.

由于安装测试新系统,计算机中心将于下周一至周三即7月1日至3日不向外开放。敬请见谅。

IV. Send a memo, in the tone of a librarian, to one of your colleagues to remind him that the book borrowed from the company's library has met the returning date.

V. Instruction: Read the question carefully. Working in pairs, draft a memo that would best present the following information.

Scenario: Your company will hold its annual Dinner and Dance (D&D) party soon. Due to the recession (poor business climate), the D&D would be scaled down. Your boss has asked you to write a memo to all staff and inform them of the upcoming D&D function.

Task: Write a memo to your company staff. Ensure that your message is clear, concise, courteous and complete. Include in your memo:

(1) Date, location and duration of the D&D.

(2) Some information on the activities that they can expect.

Some information that you might need:

Date: December 3, 2014

Venue: Orchard Parade Hotel Ballroom

Duration: 7: 00 p. m—11: 00 p. m.

Activities (some suggestions):

- Lucky Draws
- International Buffet Spread
- Singapore Idol (Karaoke competition)
- Magic Show
- Gurmit Singh aka PCK (the emcee)

Meeting Agenda

Part I Warm-up Case Study

Fasten your belt! You can begin an exciting journey towards learning to write a meeting agenda efficiently by reading the following sample meeting agenda. While studying the sample, you need to discuss its function, components, types and writing style. Finally, you are expected to explore the writing techniques on drafting a meeting agenda in a professional way. Now let's come to the following meeting agenda.

Just Us **Film**

Production Meeting Agenda

Date/Time: January 15, 2016 9:00 a. m. — 11:30 a. m.
Location: Conference Room B
Attendees:
Joshua Walker — Producer
Shara Jenkins — Writer/Director
Aren Vermont — Creative Director
Dalila Fialho — Director of Development

OBJECTIVES
- Review and finalize script
- Develop fundraising strategies for *JUST US* Film
- Finalize Pre-Production Timeline

SCHEDULE	
9:00 to 9:15	Check-in, General Updates — Aren Vermont
9:15 to 9:45	Script Review, New Changes — Shara Jenkins
9:45 to 11:00	Fundraising Updates — Dalila Fialho
11:00 to 11:15	Pre-Production Timeline — Joshua Walker
11:15 to 11:30	Announcements — All
ROLES/RESPONSIBILITIES	
Note-taking: Joshua Walker	
Mediation: Aren Vermont	

Have you got some ideas about how to write a meeting agenda after studying the above sample? If so, you are expected to do a brief analysis of the above sample and write down the key points.

KEY POINTS HERE

_____
_____
_____
_____
_____
_____
_____

Part II Having a Clear Picture

I. Concept of Meeting Agendas

A meeting agenda is an important tool for making sure meetings reach their objectives by covering the essential topics. It is to inform the participants how to prepare for the meeting by telling them what and when is to be accomplished.

II. Components of Meeting Agendas

1. Title

Start by giving your agenda a title. Your title should tell the reader two things: First, that he/she is reading an agenda, and second, what topic the meeting is covering.

2. Information in the Header.

Apart from the title, a meeting agenda usually has a header which includes "when" "where" "who" information and can vary in detail depending upon the level of formality your workplace encourages.

(1) Date and time. These can be grouped together or placed in their own separate sections.

(2) Location. If your business has multiple locations, you may want to write the address. If it has just one location, you may want to name the room you're meeting in (e.g., Conference Room #3).

(3) Attendees. Job titles are usually optional and not required.

(4) Special individuals present. These may be special guests, speakers, or meeting leaders.

3. A Brief Statement of the Meeting Objective(s)

Skip a line after your header and use bolded or underlined text to label your objective section with a title like "Objective" or "Purpose", followed by a colon or a line break. Then, in a few concise and to-the-point sentences, describe the items of discussion for the meeting.

4. A Schedule Outlining the Main Elements of the Meeting

Skip a line after your statement of the objective(s), give your schedule a bolded or underlined title, and then begin making entries that correspond to the main topics of discussion in your schedule. Label each entry with either the time you plan for it to begin and end or the amount of time you plan for each entry to take.

5. Time in the Schedule for Any Special Guests

If any guests are coming to your meeting to discuss topics of importance, you'll want to devote a chunk of the meeting time to these people. It is best to contact the guests ahead of time to figure out how much time each one will need for their discussion topic.

6. Extra Time at the End of the Meeting for Q&A

During this time, people can ask for clarification about confusing topics of discussion, offer their own adjunct opinions, suggest topics for future meetings, and make other comments.

III. Tips for Meeting Agenda Writing

An effective agenda sets clear expectations for what needs to occur before and during a meeting. It helps team members prepare, allocates time wisely, quickly gets everyone on the same topic, and identifies when the discussion is complete. Here are some tips for designing an effective agenda for your next meeting:

(1) List agenda topics as questions the team needs to answer. A question enables team members to better prepare for the discussion and to monitor whether their own and others' comments are on track.

(2) Note whether the purpose of the topic is to share information, seek input for a decision, or make a decision. It's difficult for team members to participate effectively if they don't know whether to simply listen, give their input, or be part of the decision making process.

(3) Estimate a realistic amount of time for each topic. The purpose is to get better at allocating enough time for the team to effectively and efficiently answer the questions about each topic.

(4) Identify who is responsible for leading each topic. Identifying this person next to the agenda item ensures that anyone who is responsible for leading part of the agenda knows it and prepares for it before the meeting.

(5) Check the agenda for errors before distributing it. Because some attendees may end up relying heavily on the meeting agenda, it's wise to proofread it for errors and completeness before giving it out.

Part III   Showing Your Talent Slightly

Now that you have had a clear picture of the components of meeting agenda, you can fulfill the following situational task with the help of the Warm-up Case Study.

I. Situational Task

Suppose you are the secretary of the English Department and you are required to draw up an agenda of the teacher's meeting. The purpose of the meeting is to provide training to encourage teachers to use new technology in the classroom including OneNote and smart phones.

_____
_____
_____
_____
_____
_____

II. Do It Yourself

Part IV Opening the Treasure Box

I. Samples

Sample 1

MEETING AGENDA – STAFF MEETING

MEETING INFORMATION

Objective:	Weekly updates and company news		
Date:	May 2, 2016	Location:	Conference Room A
Time:	8:00 AM	Meeting Type:	Weekly Staff
Call-In Number:	1-800-CALL-ME1	Call-In Code:	1234
Called By:	Bill Smith	Facilitator:	Bill Smith
Timekeeper:	Jim Jones	Note Taker:	Jim Jones
Attendees:	IT Staff		

PREPARATION FOR MEETING

Please Read:

Please Bring:

ACTION ITEMS FROM PREVIOUS MEETING

Item/Responsible/Due Date
1. [Item Description] / [Responsible]/[Due Date]
2.

AGENDA ITEMS

Item/Presenter/Time Allotted
1. [Agenda Item] / [Presenter Name]/[Time Allotted]
2.

NEW ACTION ITEMS

Item/Responsible/Due Date
1. [New Item] / [Responsible]/[Due Date]
2.

OTHER NOTES OR INFORMATION

Sample 2

COMMITTEE MEETING - AGENDA

MEETING INFORMATION

Objective: Weekly updates, goals, and news

Date: May 2, 2016
Time: 9:00 AM
Location: Conference Room B

AGENDA

Item/Presenter
1. Call to Order/[Name]
2. Pledge of Allegiance/[Name]
3. Welcome-Introduction/[Name]
4. Roll Call/[Name]
5. Approval of Previous Meeting Minutes/[Name]
6. Old Business
   a. [Item 1]/[Name]
7. New Business
   a. [Item 1]/[Name]
   b. [Item 2]/[Name]
8. Additions to Agenda/[Name]
9. Calendar/[Name]
10. Adjournment

NEXT MEETING

May 9, 2016, Conference Room B

OTHER NOTES OR INFORMATION

Sample 3

PTA Meeting Agenda

Date/Time: Wednesday, March 6, 2013/7:30 p.m. to 9:30 p.m.
Location: Kendall Elementary School, Teacher's Lounge
Attendees: Principal Riddell, Secretary Alena Flora, PTA President Ellen Falbo, PTA Vice President Jennie Jacoby, PTA Fundraising Chair Marge Marks, various teachers and parents

OBJECTIVES
- Discuss upcoming fundraiser to raise money for fifth grade graduation activities.
- Decide on fundraiser and assign roles.
- Choose date.

SCHEDULE
7:30 to 7:45 Welcome — Ellen Falbo
7:45 to 8:15 Discuss fundraiser ideas — Jenny Jacoby
8:15 to 8:25 Discuss possible fundraiser dates and decide on them — Ellen Falbo
8:25 to 9:00 Vote on fundraiser idea and discuss details — Marge Marks
9:00 to 9:15 Question and answer period — Ellen Falbo
9:15 to 9:30 Wrap-up — Principal Riddell

ROLES/RESPONSIBILITIES
Set-up: Jennie Jacoby
Minutes: Alena Flora
Paperwork: Alena Flora
Refreshments: Ellen Falbo

Sample 4

AGENDA

For the meeting of the Board of Directors

Wednesday March 27, 2019

At 3:00 p.m. in the boardroom

1. Apologies for absence

2. Minutes of the meeting of February 28, 2019

3. Matters arising from the Minutes

4. Reports of Chairman, Marketing Director, Company Secretary and Technical Director

> 5. Client services (Mrs. Whites to attend for this item)
>
> 6. Productivity bonuses and incentives
>
> 7. Dates of meetings during 2020—2021
>
> 8. Arrangements for Directors' Annual Dinner (September)
>
> Any other business:
>
> Items of other business must be notified to the Company Secretary in writing before the start of the meeting.
>
> The meeting will end not later than 6: 00 p.m.

II. Related Expressions

(1) correspondence   *n.*（来往的）信件（尤指公函或商业信函）

A secretary came in twice a week to deal with his correspondence.
秘书每周来两次，负责处理他的信件。

(2) actionable   *adj.*（计划、信息等）可行的，可用的

(3) synchronize   *v.* 使同步

(4) bylaw   *n.* 章程，会章

(5) adjourn   *v.* 休会

(6) board of directors   董事会

There is still only one woman on the board of directors.
董事会中仍然只有一位女性。

(7) apologies for absence   为缺席道歉

(8) arise from   由……引起（产生）

Can we begin by discussing matters arising from the last meeting?
我们是不是可以从讨论上次会议所产生的问题开始？

(9) game plan   方案，策略

The former coach blamed the defeat on no game plan and no inspiration.
前任教练把这次失败归咎于没有比赛方案和缺乏激励。

(10) adopt a resolution   通过决议

They were trying to persuade the UN to adopt an aggressively anti-American resolution.
他们正竭力说服联合国通过一项强烈反美的决议。

(11) expected attendee   预计参会人员

(12) agenda item   会议议程项目

(13) time allotted 时间分配

(14) proposed process 建议程序

(15) call to order 宣布开会

(16) roll call 点名

(17) meeting facilitator 会议主持人

(18) meeting attendees 参会人员

(19) next meeting dates and places 下次会议时间和地点

(20) due date 截止日期

III. Functional Sentences

(1) Let's settle the date and place of next meeting.
让我们确定下次会议的时间和地点吧。

(2) There are some matters arising from last meeting.
上次会议产生了一些问题。

(3) Items of other business must be notified to the Company Secretary in writing before the start of the meeting.
如有其他议题请在会议开始之前以书面的形式通知公司秘书。

(4) The meeting will end not later than 6: 00 p.m.
会议将于下午六点前结束。

(5) Be prepared to ask questions and share your initial preference and your reasoning.
请提前准备好问题，并阐述你的观点和理由。

(6) Discuss upcoming fundraiser to raise money for fifth grade graduation activities.
讨论为五年级的毕业活动筹集资金。

(7) We should move to the next topic if we want to get out of here on time.
为了能准时结束会议，让我们马上进入下一个议题。

(8) Determine projected sales goals for 2014.
确定2014年的预计销售目标。

(9) Please read attached document on weekly sales numbers prior to meeting.
请在会议之前阅读附件，了解每周销售数据。

(10) Stephen will be taking meeting minutes.
斯蒂芬将做会议纪要。

(11) This is an agenda of a work team at a non-profit organization.
这是一个非营利组织工作团队的会议日程。

(12) Discuss assignment of administrative assistants to senior and executive staff, including location of work stations.

讨论高管人员的行政助理的工作职责及工作地点。

(13) Decide fees charged by entrepreneurial organizations for services.

确定企业服务的收费标准。

(14) Approve proposed policy on job posting.

批准招聘方案。

(15) Receive information on space planning; discuss next steps.

汇集关于空间规划的信息，讨论下一步行动计划。

(16) Please bring your copy of the goal action plans to the meeting.

开会时请携带目标行动方案的副本。

(17) Items that do not require a decision at this time, but may require decision at the next meeting of the Board of Directors.

本次会议没有做出决定的事项留到下次董事会表决。

(18) Discuss managing insurance program and review a draft budget.

讨论管理保险项目并审查预算草案。

(19) Review concept paper for foundation for support of environmental programs.

审查环保项目相关支撑材料。

(20) Items that do not generally require any action.

以下会议议程通常无须进行表决。

Part V　Displaying Your Prowess Fully

I. Please write a meeting agenda according to the hints given below.

宏宇大酒店于3月8日下午2点在多功能厅召开各部门经理会议，主要议题是顾客对前台服务员的投诉问题。

II. Please try to write a meeting agenda based on the following information.

某公司拟于2019年12月2日上午9点到11点在办公楼会议室举行一次经理办公会，讨论如何满足消费者的需求，扩大公司的利润问题。

III. Please draft an agenda according to the hints given below.

公司将召开一个董事会议，请按下列提示撰写一份会议日程：

会议将于2019年7月18日星期四下午1:30在2号会议室召开。

会议安排：

1:30 ～ 1:50 讨论2019年5月8日会议的会议记录

1:50 ～ 2:30 讨论在纽约与新加坡建立分公司的可能性

2:30 ~ 3:00 决定在日本分公司的投资额
3:00 ~ 4:00 威尔·史密斯先生做2020年销售工作报告
4:00 ~ 4:30 选出新任人事经理

IV. Please translate the following conference program into English.

会议安排

11月12日 星期二
  9:00 ~ 20:00 登记报到
11月13日 星期三
  9:00 ~ 9:30 开幕式
  10:00 ~ 12:00 全体会议
  13:30 ~ 18:00 分组会议
  19:00 ~ 20:00 招待会
11月14日 星期四
  8:30 ~ 12:00 全体会议
  13:30 ~ 18:00 分组会议
11月15日 星期五
  8:30 ~ 12:00 全体会议
  13:30 ~ 18:00 分组会议
  19:00 ~ 20:00 宴会
11月16日 星期六
  8:00 ~ 17:00 游览长城和十三陵

Meeting Minutes

Part I Warm-up Case Study

Fasten your belt! You can start an exciting journey towards learning to write meeting minutes efficiently by reading the following sample meeting minutes. While studying the sample, you need to discuss its function, components, types and writing style. Finally, you are expected to explore the writing techniques on drafting the meeting minutes in a professional way. Now let's come to the following meeting minutes.

Board Meeting Minutes

Franze Co. Monthly Board Meeting
February 13, 2013
Meeting called to order at 12:00 p.m. by CEO Taylor Cooper

Members present:
Taylor Cooper, CEO
Logan Shafter, CFO
Morgan Ely, Senior Vice President, Marketing
Elyse Chan, Senior Vice President, Engineering
Joyce Comer, Senior Vice President, Consulting
Lindsay Rogan, Communication Strategist
Mark Epstein, Senior Vice President, Human Resources
Shane Hale, Engineering Specialist

Nick Mitchell, International Consulting Representative

Ryan Marke, Senior Vice President, Recruiting

Members absent:

(none)

Approval of minutes:

Motion: Approve minutes from January 14, 2013 board meeting

Vote: Motion carried

Resolved: Minutes from the meeting on January 14, 2013 approved without modification

Business:

Motion from Morgan Ely to submit the latest issue of company newsletter, *The Newswire*, for national award

Vote: 10 in favor, 0 opposed, 0 abstained

Resolved: Motion carried

Motion from Shane Hale to attain 10% more engineering materials for company

Vote: 4 in favor, 6 opposed

Resolved: Motion failed

Motion from Mark Epstein to hire 5 interviewed candidates to fill vacant positions at the company

Vote: 6 in favor, 4 opposed

Resolved: Motion carried

Meeting adjourned at 1:14 p.m. by CEO Taylor Cooper

Respectfully Sumitted,

Alice Green

Alice Green, Secretary

Have you got some ideas about how to write the meeting minutes after studying the above sample? If so, you are expected to do a brief analysis of the above sample and write down the key points.

KEY POINTS HERE

_____
_____
_____
_____
_____
_____
_____
_____

Part II Having a Clear Picture

I. Concept of Meeting Minutes

Minutes are official written records of what is said and decided at a meeting. They are prepared for the company files, for the reference of those in attendance, and for the information of absentee. Minutes are important because they keep the original and historical records of a meeting in the file. Whatever discussed and reached in a meeting can easily be traced in the minutes.

II. Components of Meeting Minutes

The format used for minutes varies from one organization to another. But a set of minutes should normally include the following information:

(1) The name of the organization;

(2) The place, date, and time of the meeting;

(3) The name of the person presiding;

(4) List of people attending;

(5) List of absent members of the organization;

(6) Approval of the previous meeting's minutes, and any matters arising from those minutes;

(7) For each item in the agenda, a record of the principal points discussed and decisions taken;

(8) Date, time and place of next meeting;

(9) The time of adjournment;

(10) Name of person taking the minutes.

III. Types of Meeting Minutes

According to their degree of formality, minutes can usually be divided into two types: informal minutes and formal minutes.

1. Informal Minutes

When a meeting does not follow the parliamentary procedure, its minutes can be quite informal. Informal minutes are to have a comprehensive summary and take down, one after another, the important events such as motions, plans and resolutions.

2. Formal Minutes

Formal minutes are those that follow the parliamentary procedure. They concentrate on the specific actions taken at the meeting, including committee reports heard and accepted and motions made, and passed.

IV. Tips for Meeting Minutes Writing

(1) Put the date, time and place of the meeting at the top of the page. This enables others to look up a particular meeting if they need to refer back to earlier business. The date and time also links a particular meeting to its minutes.

(2) Follow it with the organization's title, and frequency of the meeting — weekly, monthly or quarterly. If the minutes are for a special meeting that was called, be sure to capture this as well.

(3) Make sure it includes the names of the members who were present and whether the previous minutes were approved. It may include the titles of the officers, whether the attendee was a voting or non-voting member, or any guests who are at the meeting.

(4) The body of your minutes summarizes what took place at the meeting. You need to include all main motions and who made the motion, the number of yes and no votes, any requests for an appeal or for a motion to be tabled in separate paragraphs. New and old business would be nested here as well.

(5) Conclude with the time the meeting was adjourned, who moved and seconded the motion, and your signature as the secretary. Your signature validates the integrity of the minutes and the meeting content.

(6) Submit completed minutes for approval, whether it is by email, fax, mail or at the next meeting. It is always preferable for the members of the group or organization to receive the minutes before the next meeting so they can read over them.

(7) At the next meeting the chairperson or president calls for the minutes to be approved, asks if any corrections need to be made, accepts any valid corrections and announces that they have been approved.

Part III Showing Your Talent Slightly

Now that you have had a clear picture of the components and types of meeting minutes, you can fulfill the following situational task with the help of the Warm-up Case Study.

I. Situational Task

As the secretary of the Labor Grievances Committee of the Slate and Johnson Luggage Company, you must prepare the minutes of the monthly meeting held on September 23. Use the following notes you took at the meeting to complete the minutes.

(1) Called to order 4:00 p.m., employees' cafeteria, by Mr. Falk.

(2) Presiding: Mr. Falk; Present: Mr. Baum, Ms. White, Mr. Ben, Ms. Liu, Mrs. Sun; Absent: Ms. Pen.

(3) Correction made in minutes of previous meeting (August 21): Ms. White, not Ms. Pen, to conduct study of employee washroom in warehouse. Approved and corrected.

(4) Mr. Ben presented results of survey of office employees. Most frequent complaints agreed on. Mr. Ben presented these complaints to Board of Directors.

(5) Report on condition of warehouse employee washrooms presented by Ms. White. Accepted with editorial revision.

(6) Adjourned 5:15 p.m. Next meeting at the same time and place on October 22.

II. Do It Yourself

Part IV Opening the Treasure Box

I. Samples

Sample 1

MINUTES OF INVESTING ABROAD MEETING
Hongsheng International Trade Co. Ltd.
November 20, 2014

Presiding: Alfred Bloggs

Present: Daniel Mendoza

　　　　Eleanor Ramsay

　　　　Gouffre Berger

　　　　Hans Bussman

　　　　John Hawkwood (investment consultant)

Absent: Richard Humphries

The investing abroad meeting of Hongsheng International Trade Company was called to order at 9:00 a.m. in the conference room by Alfred Bloggs.

Daniel Mendoza presented the investment plan of 2015. He said $50 million would be invested abroad. He then introduced John Hawkwood, the investment consultant of the company.

Daniel Mendoza gave details of the proposed investment in China. On the basis of the current figures, he thought that China's position in the Asia market had been developing very fast, and it would soon be one of the main marketers in the global market.

Eleanor Ramsay argued that situation in the Asia market was changeable. She thought that future growth would be much slower.

The committee concluded that future analysis had to be carried out before a final decision was taken. Daniel Mendoza asked John Hawkwood to attend the next meeting on December 20 with a fuller analysis.

The meeting adjourned at 11:00 a.m.

　　　　　　　　　　　　　　　　　　　　　　　　Respectfully Submitted,

　　　　　　　　　　　　　　　　　　　　　　　　Emmy Lee

　　　　　　　　　　　　　　　　　　　　　　　　Emmy Lee, Secretary

Sample 2

MINUTES OF THE MEETING
OF THE EXECUTIVE COMMITTEE
OF THE YOUTH'S ASSOCIATION
June 1, 2014

Presiding: Eric Cox

Present: Hubert Latham, in the chair

       Leon Bagrit

       Louis Bleriot

       Othmar Ammann

       Bill Wilkins

       George Carlton, Secretary

Absent: Frank Halliday

The fourth meeting of the Executive Committee of the Youth's Association was held in the conference room at 36 Munan Road, at 9:00 a.m. on Friday, June 1, 2014.

(1) The minutes of the third meeting held on Thursday, June 1, 2013, were read and approved.

(2) Matters arising from the minutes. The Secretary reported that Miss Jenny Xu has accepted the post of Public Relations Officer and will assume her duties on September 1, 2014.

(3) Social Convener. The Chairman pointed out that the Association will organize a number of social gatherings in the near future. It is necessary to co-opt a Social Convener into the Committee. After considering the choice in detail, it was agreed that Susan Wenworth be co-opted as the Social Convener.

(4) Fund-raising Campaign. After a detailed discussion, it was unanimously agreed that the Association will launch a fund-raising campaign in the form of Gala Premiere in December, with a target of 20,000 dollars. Leon Bagrit and Bill Wilkins were requested to form a sub-committee and work out a plan for the next meeting.

(5) Any other business. The Secretary reported that Xinghua Bookstore has donated one hundred books to the Association. The Chairman would write a letter to thank the company on behalf of the Association.

(6) Date and place of the next meeting. The Chairman announced that the next meeting of the Committee will be held at 9:00 a.m. on Friday, June 1, 2015, in the conference room.

The meeting adjourned at 11:00 a.m.

Respectfully Submitted,

George Carlton

George Carlton, Secretary

Sample 3

MINUTES OF THE MEETING
OF THE CAPITAL IMPROVEMENTS COMMITTEE
The Mariposa Orchid Company
December 22, 2014

Presiding: David Pierce

Present: Rex Smith

John Miller

Rockne Green

Absent: David Chennault

The weekly meeting of the Capital Improvements Committee of the Mariposa Orchid Company was called to order at 8:00 a.m. in Room 512 by David Pierce. The minutes of the meeting of December 15, 2014 were read by Rex Smith and approved.

The main discussion of the meeting concerned major equipment that should be purchased by the end of the year. Among the proposals were these.

Rockne Green presented information regarding three types of laptop computers. On the basis of his cost analysis and relative performance statistics, it was decided, by unanimous vote, to recommend the purchase of IBM ThinkPad R40 laptop computers.

John Miller presented a request from the secretarial staff for new desktop computers. Several secretaries have complained of major and frequent breakdowns of their old machines.

Rockne Green will further investigate the need for new desktop computers and prepare a cost comparison of new equipment versus repairs for the next meeting.

The next meeting will be held at 8:00 a.m. on December 29, 2014, in Room 512.

The meeting adjourned at 9:30 a.m.

Respectfully Submitted,

Rex Smith

Rex Smith, Secretary

II. Related Expressions

(1) minutes　*n. (pl.)* 会议记录

(2) preside　*v.* （在正式仪式、会议等）担任主持

(3) adjourn　*v.* 休会

(4) the Labor Grievances Committee　劳工申诉委员会

(5) call to order　（保持安静）开会；保持秩序

(6) present sth. to sb.　向……提出（观点、计划等）

　　The team is presenting its report to the board on Tuesday.
　　该工作组将在星期二向董事会提出报告。

(7) be in attendance　出席，参加

　　Over 2000 people were in attendance at yesterday's demonstration.
　　有两千多人参加了昨天的示威游行。

(8) be read and approved　被审议通过

(9) co-opt sb. onto/into sth.　推举（增选）……为新成员

　　Mr. King has been co-opted onto the board.　金先生已被增选进董事会。

(10) by unanimous vote　一致通过

(11) Respectfully Submitted　（敬语，通常写在会议记录人签名的前面）

(12) motion carried　提案获得通过

(13) motion failed　提案未获得通过

(14) members present　出席人员

(15) members not present　缺席人员

III. Functional Sentences

(1) The investing abroad meeting of Hongsheng International Trade Company was

called to order at 9:00 a.m. in the conference room by Alfred Bloggs.

艾尔弗雷德·布洛格斯组织召开宏生国际贸易公司海外投资会议，会议于上午9点在会议室举行。

(2) The minutes of the third meeting held on Thursday, June 1, 2014, were read and approved.

2014年6月1日（星期四）召开的第三届会议内容已经被审议通过。

(3) Among the proposals were these.

会议提出的建议如下。

(4) Mr. Ben arranged to present these complaints to Board of Directors.

本先生计划将这些投诉提交董事会审议。

(5) The Chairman announced that the next meeting of the Committee will be held at 9:00 a.m. on Friday, June 1, 2015, in the conference room.

主席宣布下次委员会会议将于2015年6月1日（星期五）上午9点在会议室召开。

(6) The meeting adjourned at 11:00 a.m.

会议于上午11点闭幕。

(7) Meeting was called to order at 4:30 p.m. by meeting chair Jessalyn Boyce.

会议下午4点半开始，由杰斯恩·鲍伊思主持。

(8) Minutes from the meeting on August 1, 2012 approved without modification.

2012年8月1日的会议记录未经修改获得批准通过。

(9) Motion from Shane Hale to attain 10% more engineering materials for the company.

肖恩·黑尔提议公司需增加10%的工程材料。

(10) Motion from Mark Epstein to hire 5 interviewed candidates to fill vacant positions at the company.

马克·爱普斯坦提议录用5名参加面试的候选人填补公司空缺岗位。

(11) Owner Sally Honer made a motion to hold baking training seminar on February 25.

店主萨丽·霍纳提议2月25日举办一场烘焙培训会。

(12) Members accepted the proposed change and the revised minutes were adopted unanimously.

委员接受新的提议，修改后的会议记录获得了一致通过。

(13) Swanson announced that she had recently hired a new secretary, Karla Writewell.

斯旺森宣布她最近聘用了一名新秘书，卡拉·怀特威尔。

(14) The majority of members agreed on Lease-or-Buy Consultants.

大多数委员同意聘用销售顾问。

(15) Peter noted that the past three meetings had run over the intended two-hour time slot by half an hour.

彼得指出最近三次会议的时间都比计划的 2 个小时要长，超出了半个小时。

(16) He asked members to be more mindful and focused during discussions.
他要求委员们在讨论时能更专注。

(17) Both are invited back next year to give a longer presentation about our organization.
两位都受邀明年再来我们公司做一场更精彩的报告。

(18) The organization should generate revenues where possible from the materials, too.
公司也应该充分利用资源，创造更多的收入。

(19) She noted that the Center was pleased to have established a Personnel Office and introduced Mary Glynn and Cheryl Wild.
她宣布本中心刚刚成立了人事部，并向大家介绍了玛丽·格林和谢莉尔·韦德。

(20) The minutes from the September Council were approved without change.
9 月份召开的委员会会议纪要无异议通过。

Part V Displaying Your Prowess Fully

I. You work as a secretary of the company. With the help of the following transcript of the meeting, you are to write the minutes of the meeting.

Frequent meetings have to be held among the marketing team members. The following is the script of one of these meetings which was held at the headquarters of A&G Export & Import Co.

Smith Knight (SK), the manager of the marketing team and the chairman of the meeting.

Li Ping (LP), a member of the marketing team, who has just investigated the market for Little Duck cashmere sweater in Macao.

Wang Nan (WN), a member of the marketing team.

SK: Well, I'm glad you could both come. I'm sorry this meeting had to be held at such short notice, but several things have come up that we need to discuss. You both have a copy of the agenda, any objections to the minutes of our last meeting?

LP/WN: No.

SK: Good. So let's pass straight to the first item. I think we have all had a chance to study Li's report on her recent visit to Macao and the potential for penetration of the Macao market. However, it might be a good idea for you to just run over the main points of the report, Li Ping?

LP: Well, basically, the purpose of the report is to present findings and conclusions from my visit to Macao last week. This visit was aimed at investigating the potential for our

Little Duck cashmere sweater in Macao. I must stress that this was a very small scale survey and that my findings are, as yet, very tentative.

SK: So, what, in a nutshell, are your findings?

LP: Well, to be frank, I found that our Little Duck cashmere sweater does not have an ideal market in Macao. I visited a number of department stores, and in most of these stores, our products are not put on the shelves at all! Only in certain districts could I see our sweaters — the districts where people's purchasing capacity is not very high. At present, the most popular sweaters in Macao are mainly imported from European countries.

WN: But do people in Macao really need cashmere sweaters since it is so warm there?

LP: Well, our cashmere products do not sell well in Macao partly because of the warm climate, but we do have introduced cashmere with silk and cashmere with cotton products. Still people do not seem very much interested in our things. I compared our products with that from European countries and found that the main problem is not the quality but the branding and advertising of our sweaters.

SK: Do you have any suggestion to make?

LP: Well, I consulted some advertising agencies in Macao and Hong Kong. They could handle all our advertising needs from the creation of a particular image for our company to copywriting, design and layout.

WN: What about the cost?

LP: It's about 50 thousand to 80 thousand *Yuan* depending on what media we would choose. Print media advertising is more economical. Taking the feature of our products into consideration, we need to go with color separations. That adds to the cost.

SK: But if we do it with black and white advertisements, people cannot see the wide range of colors we provide.

LP: That's right. That's the cost we have to pay. But we don't need many big advertisements. That is to say, all things being equal, frequency is better than size, and the cost of running small advertisements is considerably less expensive.

SK: That makes sense. Well, Li Ping, thank you for your short briefing. No doubt, we'll come back to this subject when we have studied Li Ping's report. Now, let's move on to the next item on the agenda. Domestic marketing...

II. Read the following sample and answer the questions.

Minutes of the Meeting Held to Discuss the Sitting of the New Workshop

Date: 2:00 p.m. on April 4, 2014

Present: Peter Lee, Site Manager (chair); John Ryan, Factory Manager; Howard Vassey,

Chief Engineer; Own Smith, Chief Accountant; Carl Black, Chief Architect

Apologies for absence: Skip Cyprus, Financial Manager

The minutes of the meeting held on March 14, 2014 were read and confirmed as being a true record.

(1) Matters arising from the minutes: None.

(2) Peter Lee's proposals: The Factory Manager reported that if the new site is located in the downtown, it would mean:

a. Extra renting cost;

b. Limited space;

c. Convenient transport.

(3) Howard Wassey's report: Chief Engineer confirmed that space was limited especially in times of high production.

(4) Resolved:

a. We need to find a new site in the suburb for the workshop.

b. Final cost should be limited in $200,000.

c. We should work out the schedule for the new site which is needed by the architects.

The meeting adjourned at 4:00 p.m. Next meeting to take place: April 22, 2014.

Respectfully Submitted,

Alice Nelson (Signature)

Alice Nelson, Secretary

Questions:

1. How many persons attendded the meeting? Who are they?

2. Who wrote the minutes?

3. What was the subject of the meeting?

4. How many parts are there in the minutes?

Business Report

Part I Warm-up Case Study

Fasten your belt! You can start an exciting journey towards learning to write a business report efficiently by reading the following sample business report. While studying the sample, you need to discuss its function, components, types and writing style. Finally, you are expected to explore the writing techniques on drafting a business report in a professional way. Now let's come to the following business report.

An Investigation Report

To: Louise Wang, Personnel Manager
From: John Zhao, Office Manager
Date: January 18, 2014
Subject: Staff Lateness

Introduction
Louise Wang, Personnel Manager has requested this report on staff lateness at the new Tianjin office. The report was to be submitted to her by January 15.

Illustration
Out of 24 members of staff, 23 were surveyed about:
1. Their method of transport
2. Time taken to get to work
3. Problems encountered

Findings

1. All staff are late at least once every two weeks.

2. Ten members of staff take the subway, two take the bus, six travel by car, and five travel by bicycle.

3. Traveling time varies between 20 minutes and one hour.

4. All staff experienced problems.

(1) All members of staff experienced delays on the subway due to:

a. Signal problems;

b. Engineering work;

c. Overcrowding;

d. Poor train frequency on some lines.

(2) Members of staff who take the bus experienced delays due to traffic jams.

(3) Members of staff who travel by car also experienced delays due to traffic jams and two had problems with parking, particularly on Mondays and Tuesdays.

(4) Members of staff who travel by bicycle experienced delays due to bad weather, vehicle problems and traffic jams.

Conclusions

1. All staff using public transport are late mainly because the subway and bus services are unreliable.

2. A minority of members of staff who travel by car experienced problems with parking.

3. The office opens at 9:00 a.m. and so staff are forced to travel during the rush hour.

4. Members of staff are not leaving sufficient time for their journeys which are extended due to delays.

Recommendations

1. Members of staff should leave longer for their journeys in order to allow for delays.

2. Staff should investigate alternative routes and means of transport.

3. It is recommended that staff who travel by car and experience parking problems use the new car park in Commercial Center, which opens next week.

4. It is recommended that the Personnel Director investigates the possibility of introducing a flextime system so that staff do not have to travel during the rush hour.

Have you got some ideas about how to write a business report after studying the above sample? If so, you are expected to do a brief analysis of the above sample and write down the key points.

KEY POINTS HERE

_____
_____
_____
_____
_____
_____
_____
_____

Part II Having a Clear Picture

I. Concept of Business Report

_____
_____
_____
_____
_____

II. Components of Business Reports

A short business report is made up of two parts: heading and body. The heading consists of four lines: To line, From line, Date line and Subject line; while the body is made up of five parts: Introduction, Illustration, Discussion, Conclusion (s) and Recommendation (s).

1. Introduction

In this part, you should let the reader know what is carried in your report, that is, introduce the background relative to the report, state the subjects, purpose and method of solving the problem, and summarize the findings. It should be brief and clear.

2. Illustration

This is a presentation of what the information is based on — the way you collect or acquire information, the source of your information.

3. Discussion

This is the analysis on the facts collected. It works as a key part of the report in effecting the future strategy making, and it should describe the detailed information of a subject in an object way. If necessary, it should reason the factors, result and possible measures.

4. Conclusion (s)

A conclusion is to summarize the major findings of the report and assess the implications of evidence already presented. It can also be a reinforcement of the discussed topic or idea. Most writers present conclusions after the body because the reader feels it natural and acceptable.

5. Recommendation (s)

If the report is expected to provide reference or suggestion for strategy making, the writer should put forward his own point of view based on the evidence presented in the body of the report. Suggestions are most helpful when they are practical and reasonable. Naturally, they should evolve from the findings and conclusions.

III. Types of Business Reports

From different aspects business reports can fall into different kinds. In terms of forms, there are formal report and informal report. As far as the length of reports is concerned, it can be long report and short report. Generally speaking, a long business report, meanwhile, is a formal one. A short business report can be informal, taking the form of a letter or a memo as examples. As space is limited, only short business reports are discussed in this unit, that is to say, we deal with three types of business reports here.

1. Routine Report

A routine report is a report which describes a particular situation so as to provide information on a particular incident. It is regularly presented to upper management on the sales or production of a business.

2. Investigation Report

An investigation report is a report written on the instruction or commission of some people or body. It is drawn on the base of a close survey or investigation, aimed to provide facts and suggested solutions. For example, you may be asked to survey students on their satisfaction with a new curriculum. Your report will include what you have found in the series of researches designed for this purpose.

3. Feasibility Report

A feasibility report is one that evaluates a program or a strategy-to-be. It is based on a close study of the program and a full consideration on the advantage and disadvantage of the future effect. By outlining and analyzing several alternatives or methods of achieving business success, the feasibility report helps to narrow the scope of the project to identify the best business model.

IV. Tips for Business Report Writing

1. Be Objective and Impartial

A good report presents facts and avoids presenting the writer's subjective opinion, bias or attitude.

2. Be Consistent in Tense

In writing a business report, you should choose an appropriate tense, either past or present, and be consistent with it throughout the whole report. Failing to do so will confuse the reader and result in communication barrier.

3. Write Concisely and Express Your Ideas Exactly

Effectively writing is concise — each word, sentence, and paragraph counts. A good writer of business report normally prefers short words to long words and sentences to long ones, concrete words and sentences to abstract ones so that all the information is given in a convincing way.

Part III Showing Your Talent Slightly

Now that you have had a clear picture of the components and types of business reports, you can fulfill the following situational task with the Warm-up Case Study.

I. Situational Task

This is a report on market share of milks. The introduction and the illustration has been made. Now try to draw a discussion.

The market research was made in last May, and it was focused on the types of milk instead of their manufacturers as it was designed for our next year's production.

Our team went to the major supermarkets in Tianjin during the first two weeks of May and kept the stock recording every day. The recording shows:

(1) Full cream milk takes up 35%, almost at the same level of last year.

(2) Skimmed milk 13%, while last year it was 10%.

(3) Yogurt 38%, increased 4%. compared with last year.

(4) Fruit milk 12%, decreased 3%. compared with last year.

(5) Others 2%.

II. Do It Yourself

_____
_____
_____
_____
_____
_____
_____
_____
_____

Part IV Opening the Treasure Box

1. Samples

Sample 1

> **To:** Managing Director
>
> **From:** Personnel Manager Division A
>
> **Date:** May 14, 2014
>
> **Subject:** Proposed Installation of Automatic Coffee Machine
>
> **Introduction**
>
> Following your memo of April 25 we carried out a small study of staff views in three selected departments.
>
> **Illustration**
>
> The personnel officer informally asked office workers a representative sample of some questions. The questions included:
>
> - whether they drank coffee during their break;
> - whether they made it themselves or brought it with them from home;
> - whether they would be in favor of a shorter coffee-break;
> - whether they would use an automatic coffee machine if available.
>
> **Discussion**
>
> We can summarize the results as follows:
>
> - About 65% said they enjoyed a good cup of coffee.
> - Only 5% brought their own coffee with them from home.

- About 25% would be in favor of a shorter coffee break and finishing earlier.
- About 15% said they would use the automatic coffee machine.
- If the coffee was cheap, more could be added.

On April 28, during a routine meeting with the chief union representative, I mentioned that in some departments the coffee break was lasting a lot longer than is actually allowed. The representative's answer was not very helpful. She said the union would insist on the coffee break being left as it is. She also said without asking all union members' opinions, the union would not agree with any shortening of the coffee break.

Conclusion

In conclusion, it seems important to draw the board's attention to possible difficulties which the rapid installation of coffee machine could bring.

Recommendation

We need to discuss the problem a little longer and with more people before taking any action, and we should work out a solution with the help of the union.

Sample 2

To: Board of Directors
From: Personnel Department
Date: December 2, 2014
Subject: Flextime System

Introduction

It is requested on December 2, by the directorate who asked the Personnel Department to investigate the possibility of the firm working "flextime", and to make a report on the findings.

Illustration

1. All staff were interviewed on their needs for various time bands. Staff were then interviewed on their preferences for various time bands.

2. A questionnaire was issued to all staff asking them to state which time band they wanted.

3. The work done by the staff was observed to see if it was necessary for all staff to be present during "core time", and to ascertain precisely when this core time is.

Findings

1. Staff needs and preferences

1) Staff needs

(1) The major findings from interviewing staff on their needs were that most of the working mothers needed to be free from 3:30 in the afternoons. The reasons given were (arranged in order of priority):

  a. Collection of young children from school;

  b. Being at home when their children arrived home from school;

  c. Preparing meals for the family between the hours of 5:00 and 7:00 p.m.;

  d. About 19% of the staff are working mothers.

(2) Staff who had recently moved, or who had lived far away from the firm for some time, needed extra time to arrive punctually in the mornings.

2) Staff preferences

(1) Approximately 60% of the staff interviewed would prefer to arrive later in the morning. The periods ranged from 30 minutes to 2 hours.

(2) About 25% of the staff interviewed would prefer to finish work earlier than at present. This ranged from 30 minutes to 1 hour.

2. The firm has close communications with other firms, departments and local offices which do not operate flextime. The firm relies heavily on banking and post office services.

3. Core time

(1) Checking on the validity, accuracy and urgency of forms, documents and applications sent to the firm requires an efficient and streamlined operation. Some members of staff need to be on hand to verify cross-check and revise communications ready for signing and dispatch. This contingency did not depend on all office staff being present for consultation.

(2) The greatest volume of telephoned requests for information and advice was between the hours of 10:00 a.m. and 3:00 p.m.

(3) The least busy period was from 3:30 to 5:00 p.m., when public calls fell away, and some work was left for the following morning.

Conclusions

1. There is a conflict between 23% of staff members who need to arrive earlier in the day, and 60% who would prefer to arrive later. Most of the paperwork needs to be done earlier to be filed, signed and dispatched while senior staff are available, and also to catch the earlier postal collections.

2. The 19% of the staff — the working mothers — who need to arrive earlier and leave earlier would help to clear the backlog of work from the previous day, but they would need to be helped by the extra staff.

3. There would need to be heavy discouragement of staff wishing to arrive 2 hours and more later than at present.

4. We would need to test the degree of certainty about late arrivals. Some staff members are obviously not sure yet when they would prefer to arrive.

Sample 3

To: The Executive Council
From: Allen Taylor, Director of Operation
Date: March 26, 2014
Subject: On the Reinvestment of This Year's Profit

Introduction

This report sets out to examine how the company should reinvest this year's profit.

Alternative

The areas under consideration are:

1. The purchase of new computers
2. The provision of language training courses
3. The payments of special bonus

Evaluations

1. New computers

The majority of company computers are quite new and fast enough to handle the work done on them. Consequently, new computers would not be recommended.

2. Language training courses

The company aims to increase exports, particularly in Spain and France. Therefore, language training courses would be an excellent idea for those employees who deal with business partners and customers overseas. In addition, training courses would increase motivation: staff would enjoy the lessons and perceive that the company is investing in them. Therefore, language training courses would be an option.

3. Special bonus payments

Although special bonus payments would have a beneficial impact on motivation, they would have no direct effect on the company's operations. There are also potential problems concerning the selection of staff eligible for the payments and the setting of a precedent for future payments. Therefore, bonus payments would not be advisable.

Conclusions

1. Purchasing new computers is not necessary at present.

2. Special bonus payments may result in problem.

3. Language training courses are good for both company's operation and employees' motivation.

Recommendation

It is felt that the best solution for both the company and staff would be to invest in language training. It is suggested that the company should organize courses in French and Spanish.

II. Related Expressions

(1) routine report   日常报告

(2) investigation report   调查报告

(3) feasibility report   可行性报告

(4) market research   市场调研

(5) be designed for   为某种特定目的计划、设置

(6) full cream milk   全脂牛奶

(7) skimmed milk   脱脂牛奶

(8) core time   （弹性工作时间制中所有人员都在上班的）核心上班时间

(9) The report is based on the facts we collected.

 这份报告是基于我们搜集到的事实。

(10) Having made a close of the survey, I found...   在做了深入调研后，我发现……

(11) We attribute the facts to the following factors...

 我们将事实归因于以下几点……

(12) To sum up...   总之，……

(13) On the basis of the findings,...   基于调查结果，……

(14) Several conclusions concerning... can be drawn.   关于……的结论如下。

(15) The findings of this study indicated...   研究调查结果表明……

III. Functional Sentences

(1) This is the report about the market share of milks in the city of Tianjin.

这份报告是关于我公司各种奶产品在天津的市场占有份额。

(2) Following your memo of April 25 we carried out a small study of staff views in three selected departments.

根据您在4月25日备忘录中的指示,我们对三个部门的员工进行了一次调研。

(3) A thorough comparison promoted a decision on the third program.

在进行全面比较后,我们决定采用第三个方案。

(4) I have chosen the third among the five because it's more feasible.

我在五个可选方案中选择了第三个,因为它的可行性更大。

(5) The first program has obvious advantage over the others.

第一个方案比其他几个有明显的优势。

(6) The objective of this report is to summarize the achievements we've made as well as the setbacks we've experienced in the past year.

这份报告的目的是要总结我们在去年所取得的成就和遇到的挫折。

(7) The report examines the supply and demand of the target market and recommends some market developing approaches.

这份报告研究了目标市场的供需状况,提出了一些开发目标市场的策略。

(8) The majority of respondents (90%) thought that the system helped in meeting their personal needs, and the majority (70%) wanted the scheme to be formally introduced.

大多数人的反馈(占90%)认为该方案满足了个人需求,多数人(占70%)希望该方案能够正式实施。

(9) This document is intended to present our suggestions for your project.

这份报告是我方对你方项目的一些建议。

(10) I wrote this report because there was a need for change.

我写这份报告是因为我发现它需要改变。

(11) The purpose of this study was to determine the negative effects of stress on employees and the methods that employers use to manage employees' stress.

此项研究旨在阐述压力给员工带来的负面影响,帮助雇主找到给员工减压的方法。

(12) Data for this study were collected during the fall of 2014.

此项研究的数据于2014年秋天收集。

(13) There are three primary groups that may benefit from this study.

此项研究主要对三类人群有参考价值。

(14) Data for this study were collected using a questionnaire developed by a group of

students at Southwest Texas State University.

本研究的数据来源于西南德克萨斯州大学一组学生做的问卷调查。

(15) The respondents involved in this survey were employees working in a company located in Central Texas.

这项调查的受访者是来自德克萨斯州中部的一家公司的员工。

(16) Simple statistical techniques were used to tabulate the results of this study.

此项研究使用了一些简单的统计技术来汇总结果。

(17) This study may be limited through the use of a questionnaire as a data collection instrument.

由于此项研究只使用了调查问卷数据采集法，因此研究结果可能会有一些局限性。

(18) All attempts have been made to minimize the effects of these limitations on the study.

我们已经努力减少了对研究结果有限制作用的因素。

(19) The findings will be presented in three sections.

将从以下三个方面论述调查结果。

(20) Based on the findings and conclusions in this study, the following recommendations are made.

基于以上调查结果和结论，作出以下建议。

Part V   Displaying Your Prowess Fully

I. Draft a report according to the hints given below.

Survey your class or a group of about 20 students to determine what kinds of jobs they hope to have when they graduate. Collect and analyze the data and then make an investigation report.

II. Draft a report according to the hints given below.

There are some problems with the transport taking students to and from classes. You have been asked to investigate the situation and make some suggestions.

III. Draft a report according to the hints given below.

Your supervisor has asked you to investigate the methods used to conserve energy in three firms in your area. Assume that you have interviewed three employees of different firms. Prepare a report of your findings.

Recruitment and Employment

Job Advertisement

Part I Warm-up Case Study

Fasten your belt! You can start an exciting journey towards learning to write a job advertisement efficiently by reading the following sample advertisement. While studying the sample, you need to discuss its function, components, types and writing style. Finally, you are expected to explore the writing techniques on drafting a job advertisement in a professional way. Now let's come to the following sample.

Marketing Assistant

HaiSports is a new joint venture company, founded by the Shanghai-based sports firm Shanghai Sports & Leisure Company and the well-known British sports company Westminster Sports. HaiSports aims to sell high-quality sports equipment to both the Chinese and international markets.

There is an exciting opportunity for three new marketing assistants to join the HaiSports team. You will be responsible for helping to turn HaiSports into one of the most reputable brands in the sports equipment marketplace. You will have an active role in putting together and implementing our international marketing strategy.

You will have:

A university degree in a marketing-related discipline or at least two years of work experience in a marketing role.

Starting salary: 6000 RMB per month

> Benefits: As a HaiSports employee, you will be entitled to a 40 percent discount on all HaiSports products; plus other benefits.
>
> Please send your CV and a covering letter to:
> Grace Zhou
> HaiSports
> Penglai Lu
> Shanghai 200205

Have you got some ideas about how to write a job advertisement after studying the above sample? If so, you are expected to do a brief analysis of the above sample and write down the key points.

KEY POINTS HERE

_____
_____
_____
_____
_____
_____
_____
_____
_____

Part II Having a Clear Picture

I. Concept of Job Advertisement

A job advertisement is an announcement in a newspaper or magazine, informing people that a job is available. In other words, it is an act of seeking prospective employees or members for an organization. Recruitment is a vital function for an organization to maintain its personnel.

Job advertisement and recruitment processes should follow the classical AIDA selling format: Attention, Interest, Desire, and Action.

II. Components of Job Advertisements

1. The Name of Recruiter

For example, Swatch Group, PepsiCo (China) Co., Ltd., Nike Inc.

2. The Logotype of the Recruiter

3. The Brief Introduction to the Recruiter

—Types of organization: joint venture, sole investment enterprise, state-owned enterprise, private enterprise, international group, multinational corporation

—History and business scope

—Enterprise objective

4. The Job Titles Being Offered

For example, Sales manager wanted; Vacancy for electric engineer; Position: Bookkeeper.

5. The Job Responsibilities

For example, Project Management Assistant

Responsibility:

—Provide services for the project in Tianjin.

—Provide assistance to the project manager for everyday work.

—Responsible for file management, customer service for students and parents.

6. The Qualifications for Application

Requirements:

—College degree or above.

—Good English and computer skills.

—Related work experience in international organizations.

—Patient, careful, supportive.

—Has strong team work spirit.

7. The Remuneration Being Offered

We offer an attractive salary package, fringe benefits and good opportunities for career development.

8. The Ways of Application

Please send resume in English and Chinese, copy of certificate, ID card to the following address:

5/F, Ling Nan Hotel,

No. 22, Zhan Qian Heng RD,

Guangzhou, P. O. Code: 510010

III. Language Features of Job Advertisements

1. Creating Some Novel Headings

For example, Wanted, IBM Not Always Have Vacancies, Developing your Future, It's You who Make Everything Possible.

2. Employing Elliptic Sentences

1) Omitting the subject

Responsibilities:

—Work with Sales Manager to develop and implement sales strategies in assigned territory.

—Develop and maintain strong relationship at all levels within his/her customers' organization.

—Be alert to competitors' activities and strategies and provide input to management in timely and effective manners.

Requirements:

—Have a university degree in Telecommunication.

—Read and write English, fluent in Mandarin and Cantonese with good interpersonal skill.

—Maintain professional image for internal and external customers.

2) Omitting the verbs

Hard work and honesty a must; Able to work on the night shift; Good analytical skill;

A good command of English; University degree or professional certificate in food science;

Experience in project, sales and after-sale service coordination required;

Energetic with strong career-ambition.

3. Utilizing Various Kinds of Phrases

25—35 years of age

Good communication skills

With 5 years' experience in computer operating

Ability to work in a team under pressure

Excellent oral and written English

Available to work for a foreign company in (TEDA)

With a pleasant mature attitude

To collect prevailing market information on products and potential clients

Developing sales in northern China

4. Using Imperative Sentences Frequently

Please forward your resume and recent photo to...

Please send your full resume, educational background, recent photo, ID card copy, contact telephone No. and expected salary to...

5. Making Use of Abbreviations

F/T=foreign trade

G.M.=General Manager

HR=human resources

JV=joint venture

Part III Showing Your Talent Slightly

Now that you have had a clear picture of the components and language features of job advertisements, you can fulfill the following situational task with the help of the Warm-up Case Study.

I. Situational Task

As an office clerk in President's Office, Tian Hai Co., Ltd., you are required to finish drafting a job advertisement by your superior, Miss Huang. The information is given below.

天海公司招聘进出口部经理职务

天海公司成立于1996年。我们的目标是：提供最好的服务，成为行业领头军。通过职员与客户的精诚合作，我们将不断提高贸易质量。

职位要求：

1. 本科或以上学历。

2. 良好的沟通能力和谈判技巧。

3. 精通英语口语和书面英语。

4. 经常出差。

5. 擅长电脑操作。

6. 拥有在本行业至少五年工作经验。

职位描述：

1. 维护老客户，开发新客户。

2. 了解市场趋势，分析市场需求。

3. 制订贸易计划及预算。

我们将提供优厚薪金，其他福利和职业发展空间。

请将英文简历寄至：Tianhai_hr@job.cn

II. Do It Yourself

Import and Export Manager

_____
_____
_____
_____
_____
_____
_____
_____

Part IV　Opening the Treasure Box

I. Samples

Sample 1

Logistics Specialist

Panalpina is one of the world's leading providers of forwarding and logistics services, specializing in intercontinental air freight and ocean freight shipments and associated supply chain management solutions.

We are an equal opportunity employer and welcome applications from all qualified candidates. Information provided will be treated in strict confidence and only be used for consideration of your application for the relevant or similar post(s) within Panalpina World Transport (PRC) Ltd.

Job Description

Follow up transportation progress on all purchase items, report milestone event or any potential issue.

Ensure a good working relationship with logistic company and custom services.

Follow up the market change, prepare monthly or bi-monthly analytical market report, and make constructive suggestions for improvement.

Requirements

At least BA degree majored in import and export trading and/or logistic management related subjects.

Minimum of 3 years working experience in logistic/custom clearance, import/export manual proceeding.

Good communication skill, hard working.

Reasonable language level in English.

Certificate of custom clearance is an advantage, preferable in Qingpu Area.

An attractive salary package and good opportunities for career development will be offered.

Please send resume in English and Chinese, copy of certificate, ID card to:
Panalpina_hr@163.com

Sample 2

Area Sales Executive–West China

Founded in 1985, Xian-Janssen Pharmaceutical Ltd. has since grown into one of China's largest pharmaceutical joint-venture, becoming Johnson & Johnson's largest branch on the Mainland. Its production facilities are located in Xi'an, with offices in 28 cities; together employing more than 3000 people.

The company produces and markets high-quality products and biologics in the areas of gastrointestinal disease, neurology, psychiatry, immunology, pain control, infectious disease, and oncology. The company is also committed to providing health services and developing public health education.

Job Description

- Conduct sales business plan and budget for assigned territories
- Identify new business opportunities with West China
- Work with team on Sales & Technical seminars to the industry
- Manage and coordinate the assigned territory distributor

Requirements/Qualifications

—English/Mandarin capability

—Degree in Chemical engineering/Pharmacy/Business or related discipline

—3–5 years' experience in sales/marketing environment

—Knowledge of local pharmaceutical industry, some manufacturing experience would be advantage

—Willing to travel

—Team player, work independently, self-motivated and good communication skills

Sample 3

Air Freight Manager

DHL is the global market leader of the international express and logistics industry, specializing in providing innovative and customized solutions from a single source.

DHL offers expertise in express, air and ocean freight, overland transport, contract logistics solutions as well as international mail services, combined with worldwide coverage and an in-depth understanding of local markets. DHL's international network links more than 220 countries and territories worldwide. Some 300000 employees are dedicated to providing fast and reliable services that exceed customers' expectation.

Job Requirements

- Age between 25–35;
- Experience in air freight business (Import and Export) for at least 6 years;
- Experience in operational and customer air freight service issues;
- Good knowledge of market rates and air cargo operators/co-loaders;
- Good English for communicating with overseas offices/agents;
- Strong sales ability in order to develop air freight business in our company.

Job Responsibilities

- Assist the management in strategic planning of air freight traffics development, providing advice and information support.
- Submit monthly revenue report to the management on time.

- Extensible knowledge to major air freight booking channels. Good connections with air cargo operators which are able to create an excellent working platform.
- Strong ability in problem solving and able to work under pressure.

We will offer RMB 6000 monthly, plus other bonus.

Please send your CV in English to:

Dhl123@sohu.com

Sample 4

Wanted

Adcom (Shanghai) Co., Ltd. is a Swiss trading company.

Our mission is: Pull together for success.

With the development of business, we are now seeking highly motivated individuals to help build our future and to share our success.

Job Description

Work as Office Administration:

—Office announcement such as public holiday, phone extension, utility announcement;

—Office facility maintenance and repairing;

—Assist merchandiser with purchasing export document;

—Other tasks assigned by supervisor.

Work as Cashier:

—Prepare checks and remittance forms for signatures;

—Reconcile bank a/c statement;

—Record cash and bank accounts and prepare for cash and bank journal report;

—Issue invoices including VAT and regular;

—Any work assigned by the supervisor.

Requirements

—College degree or above;

—Major in Finance or Accounting or Foreign trade;

—1–2 years' experience in MNC;

—Excellent English in both speaking and writing;

—Proficiency with MS Office (Word, Excel & Outlook);

—Certificate of Accounting Professional is required.

Starting salary: RMB 5000 monthly, plus bonus.

Please send your full resume, educational background, recent photo, ID card copy, contact telephone number and expected salary to:

maryli@126.com

II. Related Expressions

(1) specialize in　专门从事

(2) job description　职位描述

(3) requirements/qualifications　职位要求

(4) related subjects　相关专业

(5) be skilled in/be good at　擅长……

(6) good knowledge of...　十分了解……

(7) ... years' experience in...　在……有……年经验

(8) Minimum of 3 years working experience in...　在……方面至少三年工作经验。

(9) College degree or above.　大专及以上学历。

(10) Bachelor degree or above.　本科及以上学历。

(11) willing to travel...　适应出差

(12) Frequent travel is required.　经常出差。

(13) be committed to.../be dedicated to...　致力于……

(14) fringe benefits　额外福利；（工资）津贴

(15) starting salary　起薪

III. Functional Sentences

(1) Please send your full resume, educational background, recent photo, ID card copy, contact telephone number and expected salary to:

请将你的简历、教育背景、近期照片、身份证复印件、联系方式和预期薪金寄至：

(2) Strong ability in problem solving and able to work under pressure.

很强的解决问题和抗压能力。

(3) Follow up the market change, prepare monthly or bi-monthly analytical market report, and make constructive suggestions for improvement.

紧跟市场动向，进行每月或两个月一次的市场分析，并制定建设性建议以取得更好的业绩。

(4) At least BA degree majored in import and export trading and/or logistic management related subjects.

本科学历，进出口贸易或物流管理相关专业。

(5) We will offer a competitive salary package for successful candidates. Other benefits include bonus after a qualifying period.

录用者都以浮动工资制聘用，一定期限后可享受奖金。

(6) Salary RMB 10000 and plus monthly.

月薪一万元起。

(7) As a HaiSports employee you will be entitled to a 40 percent discount on all HaiSports products; plus other benefits.

一经录用，你将可享受购买 HaiSports 产品六折和其他优惠。

(8) We offer an attractive salary package, fringe benefits and good opportunities for career development.

我们将提供优厚薪金，其他福利和职业发展空间。

(9) With the development of business, we are now seeking highly motivated individuals to help build our future and to share our success.

随着公司发展壮大，我们招募有志者共同创建公司未来，共享成功。

(10) Knowledge of local pharmaceutical industry, some manufacturing experience would be advantage.

熟悉当地医药行规，有相关生产经验优先录取。

(11) We are an equal opportunity employer and welcome applications from all qualified candidates.

我们是公平公正的雇主，欢迎所有符合条件的应聘者来我公司求职。

(12) Ensure a good working relationship with logistic company and customer services.

确保和物流公司及客户服务公司的良好工作关系。

(13) Minimum of 3 years working experience in logistic/custom clearance, import/export manual proceeding.

至少 3 年物流 / 报关及进出口操作相关工作经验。

(14) Good communication skill, hard working.

良好的沟通技能、努力工作。

(15) Reasonable language level in English.

具备一定的英语水平。

(16) Team player, work independently, self-motivated and good communication skills.
具有团队合作精神、独立工作能力、自我激励及良好的沟通技巧。

(17) Identify new business opportunities with West China.
探索中国西部的商机。

(18) Submit monthly revenue report to the management on time.
按时向管理人员提交每月营业利润报告。

(19) Strong sales ability in order to develop air freight business in our company.
为发展我公司空运业务，应聘者须具备较强的销售能力。

(20) Certificate of Accounting Professional is required.
须具备会计从业资格证。

Part V   Displaying Your Prowess Fully

I. Draft a job advertisement for a chemical company according to the hints given below.

北京宏运化学有限公司

本公司是新建的中美合资企业，生产化学产品。经北京市人事局人才市场管理处批准，现拟招聘如下人员：

会计：

——具有大学毕业文凭，最好持有"注册会计证"

——具有合资公司的工作经验

——懂英语，会电脑

秘书：

——具有大专文凭，主修英语或商科

——受过秘书技能专业培训

——能操作电脑，并能用中英文打字

录用者都以浮动工资制聘用，一定期限后可享受奖金。

申请函请用英文寄至：

北京万寿路120号   邮编：100026

北京宏运化学有限公司人事处主任收

II. Draft a job advertisement for a trade company according to the hints given below.

招聘销售经理

"众望"合资企业已有二十多年历史，现正继续扩展业务，拟对外招聘销售经理。

申请者须在 30 ~ 45 岁之间，具有一定的国内外市场营销经验。

销售经理的月薪为人民币一万元起。求职信请详述个人情况与资历。中英文各一份，寄至：

厦门鹭江道群建大厦6层"众望"人事经理收（邮编：361006）；或电子邮件发至：zhongwangpersonnel@126.com

III. Draft a job advertisement according to the hints given below.

招聘英语教师

"新希望"私立学校拟招聘专职英语教师

报酬优厚

欲知详细情况或应聘请寄：

   天津市河西区友谊路13号　邮编：300020

电话号码：022-23315566

IV. Draft a job advertisement according to the hints given below.

陶氏（Dow）化学公司是全球第五大化学公司，年销售量达200亿美元。陶氏生产化工产品、塑料和农用产品，并为164个国家的客户提供服务。陶氏在世界各地拥有员工43000人。现诚聘秘书1人。

工作职责：准备月报及有关文件，日常秘书工作

条件：英语或秘书专业，学士学位，至少两年秘书工作经验，熟练掌握英语（写和说）以及计算机技能

V. Draft a job advertisement according to the hints given below in Chinese.

诚　　聘

工程管理助理

责任：

——为重庆的工程提供服务。

——日常工作中为工程经理提供帮助。

——负责文件管理，为学员和家长们提供客户服务。

要求：

  大学程度及以上学位。

——英语和计算机技能良好。

——在国际机构组织中有过相关的工作经验。

——耐心、仔细，起配角作用。具有强烈的团队工作精神。

Job Application Letter

Part I Warm-up Case Study

Fasten your belt! You can start an exciting journey towards learning to write a job application letter efficiently by reading the following sample letter. While studying the sample, you need to discuss its function, components, types and writing style. Finally, you are expected to explore the writing techniques on drafting a job application letter in a professional way. Now let's come to the following sample.

XYZ Company
87 Delaware Road
Hatfield, CA 08065
(909) 555-5555
george.gillhooley@email.com
Oct. 21, 2009

Dear Mr. Clark,

    I am writing to apply for the position of programmer advertised in the *Times Union*. As requested, I am enclosing a completed job application, my certification, my resume and three references.

    The opportunity presented in this listing is very interesting, and I believe that my strong technical experience and education will make me a very competitive candidate for this position. The key strengths that I possess for success in this position include:

    a. I have successfully designed, developed, and supported live use applications.

> b. I strive for continued excellence.
>
> c. I provide exceptional contributions to customer service for all customers.
>
> With a B. S. degree in Computer Programming, I have a full understanding of the full life cycle of a software development project. I also have experience in learning and excelling at new technologies as needed.
>
> Please see my resume for additional information on my experience.
>
> I can be reached anytime via email at george.gillhooley@email.com or my cell phone, 909-555-5555.
>
> Thank you for your time and consideration. I look forward to speaking with you about this employment opportunity.
>
> Sincerely,
George

Have you got some ideas about how to write a job application letter after studying the above sample? If so, you are expected to do a brief analysis of the above sample and write down the key points.

KEY POINTS HERE

_____
_____
_____
_____
_____
_____
_____

Part II Having a Clear Picture

1. Concept of Job Application Letter

A job application letter is a letter of introduction attached to, or accompanying another document such as a resume or curriculum vitae. The purpose of drafting a letter of application is to introduce yourself briefly and to arouse the interest of your prospective employer to give you a job interview.

II. Components of Job Application Letters

Application letters are generally one page at most in length, divided into four parts: header, introduction, body, and closing.

1. Header

It includes the sender's address and other information, the recipient's contact information, and the date after either the sender's or the recipient's address. The final part of the header is a salutation (e.g., "Dear Hiring Managers").

2. Introduction

In this part, the applicant needs to state the purpose of writing the letter ("I am writing to apply for..."), supply some context (name the contact or mention what announcement you are responding to and, most importantly, state the position you are interested in), and then briefly summarize your qualifications ("In May of this year I will receive a BBA in Economics...") and reveal, if at all possible, why you are attracted to this position and organization.

3. Body

This part should be a description of the applicant's education, work experience and specialty. It is in this section that the applicant presents his/her advantages or qualifications for the position. Details are encouraged, but the applicant should bear in mind that exaggeration or false descriptions are not allowed in the letter.

4. Closing

This part sums up the selling points made in the body of the letter, mentions any items (including CV) you are enclosing, and expresses willingness to offer any further information that the reader may want. And you need to inquire the chance of an interview and supply the contact information.

III. Types of Job Application Letters

Generally speaking, there are two types of job application letters—application letter by graduate and application letter applied to job-changing.

1. Application Letter by Graduate

In an application letter written by graduate, the content may be dull and less luxuriant for inexperience. Therefore, the applicant should place great emphasis on education, relevant courses, social practice and awards received in the college.

2. Application Letter Applied to Job-changing

In this case, the applicant has already got experience, which is an important selling point for him/her. It is wise to emphasize previous achievements, special skills, relevant training received before. Furthermore, the applicant must tell the reason why he/she wants to change his/her job. For instance, he/she wants to obtain a more challenging one or a different circumstance.

IV. Tips for Job Application letters Writing

(1) Write a concise letter of application, no longer than one page.

(2) State how you learned about the position or the organization—a flyer posted in your department, a web site, a family friend who works at the organization.

(3) Be objective in stating your capabilities and advantages. Don't boast yourself too much otherwise you will lose the opportunity of interview for giving the reader a terrible impression.

(4) Display your attitude, personality, motivation, enthusiasm, and communication skills.

(5) Use plain English instead of bookish and unfamiliar words to express your meaning clearly.

(6) Pay more attention to the tiny aspects, such as punctuation, spelling and capital letters, to give a good first impression.

Part III Showing Your Talent Slightly

Now that you have had a clear picture of components and types of job application letters, you can fulfill the following situational task with the help of the Warm-up Case Study.

I. Situational Task

You have been working as an office clerk in President's Office, Tian Hai Co., Ltd. in the past three years. Now you plan to change your job and find a vacancy online. Therefore, you need to draft a letter of application.

II. Do It Yourself

Application Letter

_____
_____
_____
_____
_____
_____

Part IV Opening the Treasure Box

I. Samples

Sample 1

Department of Applied Physics
Tsinghua University
Beijing, 100084, China

Mar. 30, 2018

Office of Graduate Admissions
Boston University
Massachusetts, U.S.A.

Dear Sir/Madam,

 I am writing in the hope that I may obtain an opportunity to further my study in Applied Physics toward Master's degree in your university.

 My name is Li Lin, an undergraduate student of the Department of Applied Physics, Tsinghua University (China). In June, 2009, I will graduate and get my B.S. degree. I plan to continue my study and research in this field under the instructions of first class professors and in a dynamic academic atmosphere. I choose Boston University because there are a congenial team of researchers, an array of databases and research projects in your school of Physics. I believe my interests are extremely congruent with the strengths of the school. And my solid academic background will meet your general entrance requirements for graduate study.

 I will appreciate very much if you could send me the Graduate Application Forms, the Application Form for Scholarships/Assistantships, a detailed introduction to the School of Physics, and other related information. My mailing address is shown on the top of this letter.

 I am looking forward to hearing from you soon.

Best regards,
Sincerely yours,
Li Lin

Sample 2

Dear Ms. Radon,

I am very interested in talking with you about employment as a Sales Representative Trainee with Bardon Corporation, and hope you will give my candidacy strong consideration. I feel I have the necessary skills and interest to be an excellent contributor to your organization, and would like the opportunity to demonstrate this through a personal interview with your recruiter during Bardon Corporation's forthcoming recruiting schedule at Syracuse. My resume is enclosed for your reference.

Although short on experience, I am long on effort and enthusiasm. I am an outgoing, friendly individual who would enjoy building strong interpersonal relationships with valued customers. My strong service orientation and bias for action would serve your company well in response to the needs and concerns of your clients. My drive, determination and leadership abilities are well-evidenced by the following accomplishments:

—Grade Point Average of 3.7/4.0

—Fraternity President, Senior Year
　Fraternity Vice President, Junior Year
　Pledge Chairman, Sophomore Year

—Captain, Varsity Crew Team, Senior Year
　Member, Varsity Crew Team, 3 Years
　Co-captain, Varsity Swim Team, Junior Year
　Member, Varsity Swim Team, 4 Years

I would like the chance to put my energy, drive and enthusiasm to work for a company such as yours. May I have the opportunity to further discuss your requirements during a personal meeting with your representative on September 22nd?

Sincerely yours,

Nichola

Sample 3

Dear Sir,

I would like to apply for the position of Pattern Maker. I am a conscientious person who works hard and pays attention to details. I'm flexible, quick to pick up new skills and eager to learn from others. I also have lots of ideas and enthusiasm. As you can see, I have had work experience in some environments, giving me varied skills and the ability to work with many different types of people. I believe I could fit easily into your company. I think this might be the perfect for me to take on this job, because I am so interested in fashion, especially in pattern making.

  I would appreciate your time in reviewing my enclosed resume and if there is any additional information you require, please contact me. I would welcome an opportunity to meet you for a personal interview.

Yours sincerely,

Mary

Sample 4

526 Ogdon Road

Springfield, MA 28472

October 26, 2018

Dr. Sheldon P. Worthington

Vice President of Research

Farley Chemical Company

825 Skinner Blvd.

Houston, TX 28736

Dear Dr. Worthington,

  Farley Chemical Company, as one of the leaders in the field of polymer chemistry, might be interested in a seasoned product Development Chemist with a demonstrated record of achievement as a new product innovator. My credentials include an M.S. in Polymer Chemistry with over 15 years research experience in the polymer industry.

  As you can see from the enclosed resume, my reputation as a creative, innovative contributor is well supported by some 22 registered patents and an additional 18 patent disclosures. My work has led to the successful introduction of 12 new products which now account for over $250 million in annual sales revenues.

I have extensive experience in the following specialty areas:

 Organic & Polymer Specialty Chemicals:

  —Water Treatment Chemicals

  —Oil Field & Mining Chemicals

  —Consumer Products Based on Water Soluble Polymers

 Polymers, Rubbers and Plastics:

  —New Polymers and Plastics-Synthetic Approach

  —New Polymers and Plastics-Physio-Chemical Approach

My current salary is $8,200, and I have no geographical restrictions.

Should you have an appropriate opportunity available as a member of your research staff, Dr. Worthington, I would welcome the opportunity to meet with you to discuss the contributions that I might make to your new product development efforts. I can be reached during evening hours at (313)528-9735.

Thank you for your consideration, and I look forward to hearing from you.

Sincerely yours,
Walter

II. Related Expressions

(1) be congruent with   与……相适合、一致

(2) an array of   一系列

(3) in a dynamic academic atmosphere   在学术气氛活跃、浓厚的氛围中

(4) meet your general entrance requirements for   满足您对……总体录用要求

(5) hope you will give my candidacy strong consideration
  希望您能多加考虑我的情况

(6) Enclosed please find a resume and a recent photo.
  随函寄上一份简历及一张近照。

(7) in the hope that   希望能

(8) under the instructions of first class professors   在一流教授们的指导下

(9) look forward to hearing from you soon　　期待能尽快收到您的回复

(10) build strong interpersonal relationships　　建立牢固的人际关系

(11) in response to the needs　　迎合需求

(12) apply for the position　　申请……岗位

(13) additional information you require　　您需要的其他信息

(14) in the following specialty areas　　在以下特殊领域

III. Functional Sentences

(1) I am writing in the hope that I may obtain an opportunity to further my study in...
　　我提笔写这封信，希望能获得在……深造的机会。

(2) Although short of experience, I am long on effort and enthusiasm.
　　尽管我经验不多，但是我的优势在于我的努力和热情。

(3) My strong service orientation and bias for action would serve your company well in response to the needs and concerns of your clients.
　　我强烈的服务意识和行动力将能很好地为公司服务，能满足贵公司客户的要求。

(4) I would appreciate your time in reviewing my enclosed resume.
　　非常感谢您利用您的宝贵时间看我随信附上的简历。

(5) I would welcome an opportunity to meet you for a personal interview.
　　我希望能有机会跟您见面进行面试。

(6) My current salary is $8200, and I have no geographical restrictions.
　　目前我的月薪是 8200 美元，我没有地域要求。

(7) I am leaving our office to be with and care for my aged mother in a different city.
　　我为照顾住在异地的年老母亲，而申请辞职。

(8) And my solid academic background will meet your general entrance requirements for graduate study.
　　我坚实的教育背景符合您在入职条件中对学历的要求。

(9) My mailing address is shown on the top of this letter.
　　我的电子邮箱地址在这封信的顶部。

(10) I am very interested in talking with you about employment as a Sales Representative Trainee with Bardon Corporation.
　　很高兴与您谈论巴顿公司销售代表实习生招聘的事。

(11) I feel I have the necessary skills and interest to be an excellent contributor to your organization.
　　我感觉我具备了服务贵组织必要的技能并很乐意成为一名优秀的员工。

(12) My resume is enclosed for your reference.

随信附上我的简历，供您参考。

(13) I would like the chance to put my energy, drive and enthusiasm to work for a company such as yours.

我很乐意有机会把我的精力、干劲和激情都投入到像贵公司这样的公司工作中去。

(14) I am a conscientious person who works hard and pays attention to details.

我是个认真负责、努力工作、注重细节的人。

(15) I'm flexible, quick to pick up new skills and eager to learn from others.

我很灵活，善于学习新技能并渴望向他人学习。

(16) As you can see from the enclosed resume, my reputation as a creative, innovative contributor is well supported by some 22 registered patents and an additional 18 patent disclosures.

就像您在简历中看到的一样，我以创造、创新而出名；并且有22个注册专利和其余18个专利披露。

(17) I have extensive experience in the following specialty areas.

我在以下专业领域有丰富的经验。

(18) I might make efforts to your new product development.

我可以为你们的新产品开发工作而努力。

(19) I can be reached during evening hours at (313)528-9735.

您晚上拨打电话(313)528-9735就能找到我。

(20) Should you have an appropriate opportunity available as a member of your research staff?

您有适合研发人员的工作岗位吗？

IV. Model Sentences

1. Sentences for the Opening

I am applying for the position of sales manager. I believe my qualifications will meet your requirements.

Your advertisement in this morning's Journal for an adjustment manager prompted me to apply for this position.

In your advertisement for an accountant, you indicated that you require the services of a competent person, with thorough training in the field of cost accounting. Please consider me an applicant for the position. Here are my reasons for believing I am qualified for this work.

2. Sentences in terms of Salary

I'd prefer not to set as alary, but since you ask, I consider $6500 a month to be satisfactory.

It's hard for me to say what my salary should be set at, but if pressed I would have to ask for $5000 a month as an initial salary.

I don't feel that I should set my own salary, as I am happy enough to have the privilege of working for you. However, I would consider a month satisfactory compensation for my apprenticeship.

3. Sentences for the Ending

If my qualifications meet your standards, I would be happy to speak with you in person.

I would like to request an interview. You can reach me by telephone number 13000011120 between the hours of 7:00–9:00 a.m. and 5:30–9:30 p.m.

May I have the opportunity to discuss this matter further with you? My telephone number is 13000011122. You can reach me between the hours of 9:00 a.m. and 5:00 p.m.

Part V Displaying Your Prowess Fully

I. Fill in the blanks to complete the following application letter.

Class 9403

Business Administration Major

Kunming Second Commercial School

34 Cui E.Rd., Kunming 650020

June 28, 2018

Mr. Wen Qiming

Manager of Marketing Department

K&H (Chinese-Foreign Joint Ventures) Market

56 Huagang N. Rd., Kunming 650033

Dear Mr. Wen,

Ms. Huang Lijia of your company has told me that your department needs a manager assistant, and I wish to ____(1)____ the position. I will ____(2)____ commercial school next month. My outstanding record at school and some experience in business has ____(3)____ me for the work you are calling for.

I am really interested in learning business practice, and also a diligent worker and a fast learner. If ____(4)____ a chance, I am sure I can prove my worth in your company.

I will be ____(5)____ during the weekdays in the morning for any interviews you may want to give. ___(6)___ is my resume, and hoping for your immediate reply.

Sincerely yours,
×, × ×

II. Write an application letter to Ms. Kate Allen for further study in Economics Department of Edinburgh University.

III. Write an application letter according to the hints provided below.

You are looking for a position in an engineering department of a firm. As a graduate student in Mechanical Engineering Department of Qingdao University, you have participated in the Profession Training Program as Programmer Trainee. Enclose your resume with details of academic courses in your letter and ask to have an appointment.

IV. Read the following job application letter and fill in the blanks with the missing information marked from A to H.

A. May 27, 2015	B. apply for	C. additional information	D. am enclosing
E. Mr. Gilbert	F. look forward to	G. candidate	H. reached

___(1)___

Dear ___(2)___,

I am writing to ___(3)___ the programmer position advertised in Guangzhou Daily. As requested, I ___(4)___ a completed job application form, my certification form, my resume and three references.

The opportunity presented in this listing is very interesting, and I believe that my strong technical experience and education will make me a very competitive ___(5)___ for this position. The key strengths that I possess for success in this position include:

a. I have successfully designed, developed, and supported live use applications.

b. I strive for continued excellence.

c. I provide exceptional contributions to customer service for all customers.

With a B.S. degree in Computer Programming, I have a full understanding of the entire life cycle of a software development project. I also have experience in learning and excelling at new technologies as needs.

Please see my resume for ___(6)___ on my experience.

I can be ___(7)___ anytime via my cell phone, 15808808888. Thank you for your time and consideration. I ___(8)___ hearing from you as soon as possible to arrange time for an interview.

Sincerely yours,
James Peng

V. Complete the following job application letter with the expressions given below.

A. I am willing to do whatever the job requires.
B. to round out my skills and knowledge
C. to be an excellent match
D. I would certainly be eager
E. I worked my way into my current position as
F. to find a position in
G. with my background and skills
H. an opening for
I. from the bottom up
J. I have developed many comparable abilities

678 SW Madison Street
Kewanee, IL61433
January 24, 2015

STANLEY COMMUNICATIONS COMPANY
P. O. Box 12345

Allow me to introduce myself:

In response to your advertisement for a Corporate Communication Assistant, I believe you will find my background and skills ___(1)___.

Believe it or not, ___(2)___ Writer/Editorial Assistant for a prestigious newspaper publication company ___(3)___. I started out as the Mascot; dressed in yellow tights and wrapped up in a newspaper. Definitely not the most dignified position I have ever held, but it does show that ___(4)___.

Having recently obtained my B.A. in Corporate Communications ___(5)___, I would like ___(6)___ a corporate setting where my strong communication skills could be of value. As you will see on the enclosed resume, ___(7)___ through my long-term employment with the California Press.

If you have ___(8)___ an enthusiastic communications professional ___(9)___, please contact me. Although I prefer to avoid the mascot gig again. ___(10)___ to discuss any related communications or PR position that would match my abilities.

Sincerely,
James Dean

Rèsumè

Part I Warm-up Case Study

Fasten your belt! You can start an exciting journey towards learning to write a resume efficiently by reading the following sample resume. While studying the sample, you need to discuss its function, structure, types and writing style. Finally, you are expected to explore the writing techniques on drafting a resume in a professional way. Now let's come to the following sample.

RESUME

Name: Zhu Lin
English name: Adam

Objective:
To obtain a challenging position as a sales manager for overseas market.

Personal data:
Gender: Male
Email: Zhulin@job.com
Office phone: 022-65597777   Mobile: 13600680007

Educational Background:
1995.7-1999.6   Nanjing Normal University   Major: English
1999.7-2002.6   Shanghai Foreign Trade Institute   Major: International trade

---

Academic Main Courses:
Management, Marketing, International Trade, Import/Export Business, Foreign Trade, College English, Computer Skill

Skills:
English: Have a good command of both spoken and written English.
Computer abilities: Skilled in use of windows / office 2000

Self-assessment:
Good professional skills, team work spirit, high liability and attribution, nice characters, self-motivated, respond well in high-pressure atmosphere, energetic, adaptable and able man, cooperative and honest to others

Employment Experience:
2002.2–2005.6 Wujiang Jinfeng Wood Door Co., Ltd.
                Managed overseas market business.
2005.7–present Dongguan Jinzhong Electric Co., Ltd.
                Managed all exporting business.

References:
Available upon request.

Have you got some ideas about how to write a resume after studying the above sample? If so, you are expected to do a brief analysis of the above sample and write down the key points.

KEY POINTS HERE

_____
_____
_____
_____
_____
_____
_____
_____

Part II Having a Clear Picture

I. Concept of Resume

A resume or curriculum vitae is a short written account of the main events of one's life. It is often required when one applies for a job. A simple resume is a summary typically limited to one or two pages of size A4 or Letter-size highlighting only those experiences and credentials that the author considers most relevant to the desired position. US academic CVs are typically longer.

II. Components of English Resumes

A resume usually includes the following items:

1. Name

Unlike most westerners, we Chinese put our family name at the beginning as surname. To avoid misunderstanding, you may either put a comma after your surname — Wang, Ming or capitalize every letter of it like this — WANG MING.

2. Address

If you like, you may write both your business or temporary address and your home address.

3. Telephone

(O) or (W) is put after your office telephone number and (H), your home telephone number.

4. Marital Status

Single or Married (no/two children) is filled.

5. Education

Schools should be listed either in chronological order (usually starting from the year when you entered college or when you got your first degree) or from the most recent backwards with the dates of attendance. Whichever way you choose, be sure that the items under the headings, such as work experience, awards and publications follow the same order.

6. Professional/Work Experience

In addition to the period of employment, you need to state your position/title, the name of the institution and your duties.

7. References/Referees

References are to offer information about your work experience or recommendation. The normal number of references is two or three, and it is imperative that you obtain their permission before using their names. In addition to names of your references, their positions, full addresses and telephone numbers are included.

III. Types of Resumes

Resumes may be organized in different ways:

1. Reverse Chronological Resume

A reverse chronological resume enumerates a candidate's job experiences in reverse chronological order, generally covering the last 10 to 15 years. In using this format, the main body of the document becomes the Professional Experience section, starting from the most recent experience going chronologically backwards through a succession of previous experience.

2. Functional Resume

A functional resume lists work experience and skills sorted by skill area or job function. It is used to assert a focus on skills that are specific to the type of position being sought. This format directly emphasizes specific professional capabilities and utilizes experience summaries as its primary means of communicating professional competency.

3. Combination Resume

A resume organized this way typically leads with a functional list of job skills, followed by a chronological list of employers. The combination resume has a tendency to repeat itself and is therefore less widely utilized than the other two forms above.

4. Online Resumes

Job seekers are finding an ever increasing demand to have an electronic version of their resume available to employers and professionals who use Internet recruiting at any time. Internet resumes differ from conventional resumes in that they are comprehensive and allow for self-reflection. Unlike regular two-page resumes, which only show recent work experience and education. Internet resumes also show an individual's skill development over his or her career.

Part III Showing Your Talent Slightly

Now that you have had a clear picture of the components and types of resumes, you can fulfill the following situational task with the help of the Warm-up Case Study.

I. Situational Task

As an office clerk in President's Office, Tian Hai Co., Ltd. for three years, you plan to change your job when you find a job vacancy on a job advertisement online. The information is given below.

Requirements for a secretary:

(1) Bachelor degree or above.

(2) Skilled in communication and negotiation.

(3) Excellent English ability both in oral and written.

(4) Good at computer skills.

(5) With at least one year's working experience in the related field.

II. Do It Yourself

Resume

_____
_____
_____
_____
_____
_____
_____
_____

Part IV Opening the Treasure Box

I. Samples

Sample 1

Resume

Name: Luo, Lina

Address: Dept. of History

　　　　　Central Institute for Nationalities

　　　　　Beijing, 100081

　　　　　People's Republic of China

Telephone: 8842-0326

Mobile Phone: 1300133333

Date of Birth: January 2, 1963

Educational Background:

　　　1983-1987　People's University, Beijing

　　　　　　　　Major: History

　　　1993-1995　University of Hawaii at Manoa

>   Major: History
>   1997-2001   Central Institute for Nationalities, Beijing
>   Major: Ethnology
>   Received Ph.D. in Ethnology, July 2001
> Languages: English, fluent in spoken and written Japanese and French,
>   able to read
> Professional Experience:
>   1987-1997   Assistant, Lecturer of History,
>   Central Institute for Nationalities
>   2001-Present Associate Professor of Sociology
>   Central Institute for Nationalities
>   Courses offered: Introduction to Sociology, Ethnology, and Policies
>   on Nationalities
> Awards and Scholarships:
>   1987   "Excellent Student", People's University
>   1990   "Outstanding Teacher", Central Institute for Nationalities
>   1997   Recipient of Wu Wenzao Scholarship, Central Institute for Nationalities

Sample 2

> **Resume**
>
> NAME: Mike Lee
> ADDRESS: 1/F, Hang Lung Bank Bldg.
>   46–48 Granvill Rd.
>   Tsimshatsui, Kowloon
> TELEPHONE: 721-1428
> DATE OF BIRTH: Aug. 8, 1968
> MARITAL STATUS: Single
> CITIZENSHIP: U.S.
> EDUCATION:
>
> Graduated   Master of Business Administration
> August 2000   University of Central Florida,
>   Orlando, Florida 32816
> Graduated   Bachelor of Business Administration
> April 1994   East Michigan University,

Ypsilanti, Michigan 48197

WORK EXPERIENCE:

April 2001　　International Education Services Hong Kong
to
Present　　　Instructor
　　　　　　　Conduct education classes at different businesses at various locations.
　　　　　　　Classes include: English Language, International Business,
　　　　　　　Negotiation Skills, and Financial Statements.

August 1998　Tasco, Maitland, Florida
to　　　　　　Vice President of Operations
April 2001　　Responsible for complete operation of all home building and home remodeling activity. Duties included setting up budget, hiring subcontractors, materials estimation, purchasing of materials, budget maintenance, and review of financial statements.

October 1994　U.S. Home Corporation, Mainland, Florida
to　　　　　　Manager
July 1998　　 Responsible for complete management of construction site. Duties included setting up budget, hiring of subcontractors (scheduling, quality assurance and budget control), materials estimation, and review of financial statements at job completion.

LANGUAGES:　Spanish, spoken and written (fluent) French
INTEREST:　　Cycling, traveling, fishing, language studies
REFERENCES:　Available/Furnished upon request

Sample 3

Resume

Personal Information:

Name: Wang Bin

Date of Birth: July 12, 1971　　Birth Place: Beijing

Gender: Male　　　　　　　　　Marital Status: Unmarried

Telephone: (010)62345678　　　Mobile: 13333221122

E-mail: 111job@sohu.com

Work Experience:

Nov. 1998–present CCIDE Inc. as a director of software development and web publishing. Organized and attended trade shows (Comdex 99).

Summer of 1997 BIT Company as a technician, designed various web sites. Designed and maintained the web site of our division independently from selecting suitable materials, content editing to designing web page by FrontPage, Photoshop and Java as well.

Education:

1991–August 1996   Dept. of Automation, Tsinghua University, B.E.

Achievements & Activities:

President and Founder of the Costumer Committee

Established the organization as a member of BIT

President of Communications for the Marketing Association

Representative in the Student Association

Computer Abilities:

Skilled in use of MS FrontPage, Win 95/NT, Sun, JavaBeans, HTML, CGI, JavaScript, Perl, Visual Interdev, Distributed Objects, CORBA, C, C++, Project 98, Office 97, Process, Pascal, PL/I and SQL software

English Skills:

Have a good command of both spoken and written English.

Passed CET-6, TOEFL: 623; GRE: 2213

Others:

Aggressive, independent and able to work under a dynamic environment. Have coordination skills, teamwork spirit. Studious nature and dedication are my greatest strengths.

Sample 4

Resume

PERSONAL INFORMATION:

Ning Lin

15/F, TOWER 2, BRIGHT CHINA,

BUILDING1, BEIJING.

OBJECTIVE:

To contribute customer relations and administrative skills to a challenging post in a hotel.

SUMMARY OF QUALIFICATIONS:

Developed interpersonal skills, having dealt with a diversity of clients, professionals and staff members.

Detail-and goal-oriented.

Function well in high-stress atmosphere.

Knowledgeable on both EECO and APTEC computers systems.

CAREER HISTORY:

1992–Present THE OLIVER HOTEL, Whitewater, KS

Worked as a Hotel Clerk

Resolved guests' needs. Controlled reservation input utilizing EECO computer system. Handled incoming calls. Maintained daily reports involving return guests, corporate accounts, and suite rentals. Inspected rooms.

1988–1991 WALDEN HOTEL, Walton, KS

Worked as a Hotel Clerk

Trained personnel. Handled telephone, international fax and telex bookings. Maintained daily and monthly reports tracking demands and guaranteed no-show billing. Utilized APTEC computer for inputting group booking and lists.

1986–1987 WALDEN HOTEL, Walton, KS

Worked as a Sales Associate

Assisted customers. Maintained stock. Opened/closed shop. Tracked best-selling novels, and made recommendations to customers.

EDUCATION:

BETHANY COLLEGE, Lindsborg, KS

Bachelor of Science; Sociology, 1983

REFERENCES:

Furnished upon request.

II. Related Expressions

(1) Professional Experience/Career History/Employment Experience/Working Experience 工作经历

(2) available/furnished upon request 按要求可提供相关材料

(3) skilled in use of   擅长使用……

(4) fluent in spoken and written Japanese and French
    日语、法语口头表达流利，笔头能力强

(5) respond well in high-pressure atmosphere   能适应高压环境

(6) good professional skills   良好的专业技能

(7) teamwork spirit   团队精神

(8) Academic Main Courses   主修课程

(9) courses offered   所学课程

(10) high liability and attribution   高度的责任感和归属感

(11) professional experience   专业经验

(12) Associate Professor   副教授

(13) negotiation skills   谈判技巧

(14) purchasing of materials   材料采购

(15) detail-and goal-oriented   注重细节和目标的

III. Functional Sentences

(1) Have a good command of both spoken and written English.
    有良好的英语口语和书面表达能力。

(2) Studious nature and dedication are my greatest strengths.
    好学、奉献是我最大的特点。

(3) Strong knowledge of general accounting procedures.
    通晓一般会计程序。

(4) Ability to work under pressure in a fast-paced environment and manage multiple tasks.
    适应快节奏、有压力的工作环境，可以处理复杂的业务。

(5) Ability to work independently with good organizational and communication skills.
    有很好的组织和表达能力，可以独立完成任务。

(6) Experience working for a large corporation.
    有在一家大公司工作的经验。

(7) Courses offered are Introduction to Sociology, Ethnology, and Policies on Nationalities.
    所提供课程有社会学概论、民族学以及国家策略。

(8) Responsible for complete operation of all home building and home remodeling activity.
    负责家庭建筑和家庭重塑活动的全部操作。

(9) Duties included setting up budget, hiring subcontractors, materials estimation,

purchasing of materials, budget maintenance, and review of financial statements.

职责包括建立预算、雇用分包商、材料估算、材料采购、预算的维护和财务报表的审阅。

(10) Conduct education classes at different businesses at various locations.

在不同地点的不同企业开展教育课程。

(11) Aggressive, independent and able to work under a dynamic environment.

积极进取，独立性强，能够在动态环境下工作。

(12) Have coordination skills, teamwork spirit.

有协调能力及团队合作精神。

(13) To contribute customer relations and administrative skills to a challenging post in a hotel.

在酒店具有挑战性的岗位上发展客户关系及管理技能。

(14) Developed interpersonal skills, having dealt with a diversity of clients.

具有良好的人际交往能力，与各种各样的客户打过交道。

(15) Resolved guests' needs.

解决顾客的需求。

(16) Handled incoming calls.

处理来电。

(17) Maintained daily reports involving return guests, corporate accounts, and suite rentals.

维护有关回头客、公司账款及套房出租的每日报告。

(18) Tracked best-selling novels, and made recommendations to customers.

追踪最畅销小说并为客户作推荐。

Part V   Displaying Your Prowess Fully

I. Fill in the blanks to complete the following resume.

Resume

Gary Wilson
809 West Cayuga St.
Philadelphia, PA 19037
(813)555-6026

_____(1)_____

Position as a Nurse of Health Care Provider.

_____(2)_____

St. Mark's Hospital, Philadelphia, PA

Surgical Nurse, 1994 to Present

Served as a staff surgical nurse. Provided health care checks for a diverse population. Performed blood pressure tests for community health outreach programs, provided a wide range of services including women's health clinic services and care for elderly patients.

_____(3)_____

B.S., Nursing, 1994

University of Scranton, Scranton, PA

References

_____(4)_____

II. An International Trade Company is going to hire a sales representative. Please write a resume for yourself.

III. A private school is looking for an English teacher. Try to make a resume according to the common requirements for an English teacher.

IV. Taking into account Ms. Wang's previous experience in Mei Yue Leather Wares Import & Export Co., Ltd., and her self-introduction, help her produce an effective resume.

My name is Wang Mei. I am a senior student in the English Department of Guangdong Institute of Science and Technology. My major is Business English. I have obtained intermediary BEC certificate and passed National Computer Test Level 2. There are four members in my family: my father, my mother, my younger brother and I. I am a happy girl who likes singing. And I have a good voice, too. I have always dreamed of becoming a super star. But life is not all about dreams. After graduation, I hope I can find a job in a big company. I think I may begin my career as a secretary. I wish I will become a successful business woman after several years!

V. Write a resume of your own.

Unit 10

Letter of Recommendation

Part I Warm-up Case Study

Fasten your belt! You can start an exciting journey towards learning to write a letter of recommendation efficiently by reading the following sample letter. While studying the sample, you need to discuss its function, components, types and writing style. Finally, you are expected to explore the writing techniques on drafting a letter of recommendation in a professional way. Now let's come to the following sample.

> To whom it may concern:
>
> As a VP Sales and Marketing at ABC Corporation, I am pleased to recommend to you my business associate Johnson Smith. I have worked closely with Johnson for more than six years and I am very impressed with his work.
>
> As the Associate Director of Engineering and Research, Johnson has managed the engineering design of more than fifty ABC products. His work is one of the major factors in continued growth of our company. Johnson has not only managed the engineering team so well, but he has also worked very closely with other teams like sales and marketing to understand the customers' needs. He is the inspiration for the team. Johnson was also involved in development of more than 20 products from scratch to end product and I would say he has done his job more than wonderfully.
>
> It is really sad for us all to see Johnson leave. But we understand that Johnson must leave us so that he can relocate to Shanghai and stay with his aging parents. I would whole heartedly and without any reservation recommend John to you. I am sure he will be a

> tremendous asset to your company.
>
> Sincerely,
> Tom Carl
> Vice President, Sales and Marketing
> ABC Corporation

Have you got some ideas about how to write a letter of recommendation after studying the above sample? If so, you are expected to do a brief analysis of the above sample and write down the key points.

KEY POINTS HERE

_____
_____
_____
_____
_____
_____

Part II Having a Clear Picture

I. Concept of Letter of Recommendation

A letter of recommendation is a letter in which the writer assesses the qualities, characteristics, and capabilities of the person being recommended in terms of his/her ability to perform a particular task or function. Recommendation letters are almost always specifically requested to be written about an applicant, and are therefore addressed to a particular requestor. Letters of recommendation are typically related to employment, admissions to institutions of higher education or scholarship eligibility.

II. Components of Letters of Recommendation

1. Salutation

The phrase "To whom it may concern" is often used here.

2. Introduction

This is your opening statement. You need to state your purpose with the first sentence. Then you are supposed to show the relationship between you and the recommended.

3. Body

This part should include specific examples and traits related to the applicant. The more relevant you can make these examples to the position being pursued, the better it will be.

4. Conclusion

In the end, you need to offer your specific recommendation, show your confidence in the individual and reiterate any final points you feel necessary.

III. Types of Letters of Recommendation

Generally speaking, there are three types of recommendation letters.

1. Employment References

A professional recommendation letter given for employment reasons is best done so by a boss or supervisor. They should provide an overall analysis of the abilities of the individual. This letter should save the future employer the time and trouble of calling to do a reference check.

2. Character References

A reference letter is given by a close friend, relative or an associate. It is to help vouch for an individual's personal qualities. They are able to meet a variety of needs.

3. Academic References

A reference letter given by a teacher, professor or trainer. These types of letters should deal with one's aptitude, curiosity and ability to perform in an academic setting. An academic recommendation should include the information about the individual that are not necessarily gained by looking over test scores and transcripts.

IV. Tips for Letters of Recommendation Writing

(1) Do not handwrite the letter but type it. Handwriting a letter is a sign that you are not serious about the task and will reflect poorly on the applicant.

(2) Remember to use official letterhead, to sign the letter, and to include both complete contact information. When you have folded the letter and put it in an envelope, sign across the seal.

Part III Showing Your Talent Slightly

Now that you have had a clear picture of the components and types of letters of recommendation, you can fulfill the following situational task with the help of the Warm-up Case Study.

I. Situational Task

As the director of President's Office, Tian Hai Co., Ltd., you got a request from Li

Xin to write a letter of recommendation for him. He has worked as a staff assistant in the company for three years and made great contribution to work in the office. Try to finish it according to the request.

II. Do It Yourself

Letter of Recommendation

_____
_____
_____
_____
_____
_____
_____
_____
_____
_____
_____
_____

Part IV Opening the Treasure Box

I. Samples

Sample 1 Letter of Recommendation for Graduate School

> To whom it may concern,
>
> As the Principal of Saint Jones High School, I am pleased to recommend to you a member of our teaching staff, Mr. John Karter, and to write this letter on his behalf for his graduate degree. John has been teaching English in the school from the last four years. He is one of our most popular and effective teachers in the school.
>
> John Karter is a highly professional gentleman. Reaction to John's English classes has been overwhelmingly positive and he himself is in love with English literature. More than once it has been reported to me that students have been spotted lingering outside the door to John's classroom listening to his lessons. John's character impact can be even seen in parent-teacher meetings.

It will be a sad day when John will leave our school for pursuing his graduate degree. We hope that he finishes his diploma and keeps his promise to return to us.

Yours sincerely,
Harry Carlson
Principal
Saint Jones High School

Sample 2 Character Letter of Recommendation

To whom it may concern,

I am very pleased to write to you a character reference for my friend John Karter.

John and my son got to same school and are very good friends. I've known John for seven years. I have always been amazed by seeing John's level of enthusiasm for any work. He gets involved in all the community activities and impresses people quite easily. He is very hard-working and always more than ready to help anybody with anything he can. There have been many incidences where he has proved all these qualities.

I would certainly recommend John for any task where enthusiasm, reliability, hard work and trustworthiness are valued.

Sincerely,
Mary Lee

Sample 3 Letter of Recommendation for Employment

To whom it may concern,

It is with great privilege that I write to you in recommendation of Marty Molly. Until recently, I have been Marty's direct supervisor. I have found him to be a pleasant, generous person who is never afraid to take on a challenging task. He has been one of our most dedicated employees.

Marty is an independent, self-directed person who is able to communicate effectively and meet even the most demanding challenges. During his three year tenure here, he set an unprecedented record in portfolio growth.

While his performance on the job has been nothing less than stellar, Marty has also become a close friend to many of us. We pride ourselves on our corporate values and close knit community, and in this area he truly shines. Marty, along with his father George, have organized many family picnics complete with story-telling and live music. Marty is not only gifted in his uncanny ability to foresee growth opportunities, he is also a very talented musician!

Though we are all deeply disappointed to lose Marty, I highly recommend him for employment with your organization. He is a team player, a great person and an absolute financial genius.

Best Regards,

Scrooge McDuck
President
McDuck Financial Services

Sample 4 Letter of Recommendation for Employment

To whom it may concern,

This letter is to serve as my formal recommendation for Andrew Fuller. Andrew has been my direct assistant for several years. He has been interested in obtaining an MBA degree for some time now and I feel that he would be an excellent candidate for your esteemed program.

During his time here, Andrew has consistently demonstrated a strong work ethic and a dedication to success. His efforts have produced high quality results time and time again. Last year, Andrew developed and successfully implemented a plan to streamline our production department. The plan was a major undertaking, requiring a great deal of thought and effort on Andrew's behalf.

Though Andrew is my assistant, he is also in an unofficial leadership role. Many of his co-workers seek his advice and support. Andrew is always there for them and is quite comfortable in the role. I feel his budding leadership abilities will become even more effective in a business school setting.

For these reasons, I highly recommend Andrew Fuller as a candidate for your MBA program. If you have any questions regarding Andrew or this recommendation, please

> contact me.
>
> Sincerely,
John Thomas
Operations Manager Tri-State Directorie

II. Related Expressions

(1) offer one's assistance　　提供帮助

(2) community activities　　社区活动

(3) take on a challenging task　　承担挑战性的任务

(4) get involved in　　参与

(5) demonstrate a strong work ethic and a dedication
    证明具有很强的职业道德和奉献精神

(6) seek one's advice and support　　寻求某人的建议和支持

(7) budding leadership abilities　　崭露头角的领导能力

(8) on one's behalf　　为……的利益，代表

(9) be pleased to　　乐于……

(10) be disappointed to do　　做某事感到很失望

(11) financial genius　　金融天才

(12) serve as　　为……服务

(13) work ethics　　职业道德

(14) To whom it may concern　　致有关方

(15) highly recommend　　高度推荐

III. Functional Sentences

(1) It is with great privilege that I write to you in recommendation of...
    我很荣幸致信向您推荐……

(2) I would like to recommend... as a candidate for a position with your organization.
    我很高兴向您推荐……作为贵公司该职位的候选人。

(3) I am pleased to recommend to you my friend...
    我很高兴向您推荐我的朋友……

(4) He did an excellent job in this position and was an asset to our organization during his tenure with the office.
    他本职工作出色，他在任职期间是我们公司不可多得的人才。

(5) I feel that he would be an excellent candidate for your esteemed program.
　　我认为他将是贵项目中出色的候选人。

(6) If you have any questions regarding... or this recommendation, please contact me.
　　如果您对……和这封推荐信有任何的问题，请您联系我。

(7) He is one of our most popular and effective teachers in the school.
　　他是我们学校最受欢迎和最具影响力的老师之一。

(8) John's character impact can be even seen in parent-teacher meetings.
　　约翰的性格影响力可以在家长教师会上显现出来。

(9) It will be a sad day when John will leave our school for pursuing his graduate degree.
　　约翰离开学校攻读他的研究生学位时会是伤感的一天。

(10) We hope that he finishes his diploma and keeps his promise to return to us.
　　我们希望他完成学业时会履行承诺回到我们学校。

(11) I have always been amazed by seeing John's level of enthusiasm for any work.
　　我为约翰对任何工作的激情感到惊讶。

(12) I have found him to be a pleasant, generous person who is never afraid to take on a challenging task.
　　我发现他是一个乐观、大方从不畏惧挑战的人。

(13) This letter is to serve as my formal recommendation for Andrew Fuller.
　　这封信是作为我对安德鲁·福勒的正式推荐。

(14) His efforts have produced high quality results time and time again.
　　他的努力一次又一次取得了很好的成果。

(15) I highly recommend Andrew Fuller as a candidate for your MBA program.
　　我强烈推荐安德鲁·福勒作为你们MBA项目的候选人。

(16) He is also in an unofficial leadership role.
　　他还担任非官方机构的领导。

(17) He is a team player, a great person and an absolute financial genius.
　　他能适应团队工作，是个伟大的人也是个金融天才。

(18) Many of his co-workers seek his advice and support.
　　很多他的同事都喜欢征求他的意见和支持。

(19) It is with great privilege that I write to you in recommendation of Marty Molly.
　　为马蒂·茉莉写推荐信是我的荣幸。

(20) He is very hard-working and always more than ready to help anybody with anything he can.
　　他很努力工作而且随时准备帮助别人。

Part V Displaying Your Prowess Fully

I. Draft a letter of recommendation for employment.

II. Your friend, Tom, requests a letter of recommendation from you. Please draft a Character Recommendation Letter for him.

III. Draft a letter of recommendation for Graduation School.

IV. Read the following letter of recommendation and then fill in the blanks with the expressions given below.

A. Jane possess many other qualities
B. has demonstrated an eagerness to learn
C. I recommend her without reservation
D. I have been very impressed
E. were instrumental to
F. In conclusion
G. possesses an excellent grasp for
H. The character and work ethic

To whom it may concern,

I have worked very closely with Jane Doe both as a supervisor while she worked in the Career Office and as an advisor. During this time ____(1)____ by the dedicated manner with which Jane carried out her work assignments and pursued her academic coursework. Jane has displayed a maturity, motivational level and seriousness of purpose which I have rarely encountered during my extensive interactions with college students. Jane is very bright and ____(2)____. She is a quick study and has shown the ability to grasp general principles as well as subtle details.

____(3)____ which I believe will make her a very successful student of the Law. She is very well organized, approaches projects in systematic way, and manages her time effectively. Gathering information and producing quality documents ____(4)____ Jane's success while working in the Career Office. Ms. Doe ____(5)____ the English language and displays effective writing and editing skills through her work.

____(6)____, Jane Doe is an outstanding young woman who has a very strong interest in studying the law. She ____(7)____ that I am confident will lead to success in her legal studies and subsequent legal career. Ms. Doe left ABC College as a well respected student and solid member of the community. ____(8)____ for a spot in your incoming class of law students.

Please feel free to contact me if you need further information.

Sincerely,
Zhe Peng
Director, Career Office
518-580-5888
email@college.edu

V. Put the following sentences into the right order and make them a complete letter of recommendation.

A. Sincerely yours,

B. Dear Sir/Madam:

C. Based on his excellent undergraduate work and his outstanding performance here, I believe Ali will perform well in graduate school. I recommend his acceptance to your MBA program.

D. I am happy to write on behalf of Ali Cavanaugh, candidate for admission to Harvard's MBA program. Ali joined our company immediately after his graduation in Marketing from the University of North Carolina. He has been with us for three years.

E. Because of his good performance, Ali received several promotions at our company. However, his lack of confidence as a speaker prevented him from receiving some high-level positions for which he was otherwise well qualified. I believe Harvard's emphasis on classroom participation in public speaking.

F. Ali held an important position in the Department of Consumer Service. He was responsible for answering letters from our consumers, and he managed this task with skills and professionalism. Ali was an excellent writer who consistently demonstrated an understanding of consumer needs and corporate image.

G. Human Resources Manager

H. John Smith

Corporate Promotion

Corporate Profile

Part I Warm-up Case Study

Fasten your belt! You can start an exciting journey towards learning to write a corporate profile efficiently by reading the following sample corporate profile. While studying the sample, you need to discuss its function, structure, types and writing style. Finally, you are expected to explore the writing techniques on drafting a corporate profile in a professional way. Now let's come to the following sample.

Hongyun Import & Export Co., Ltd.

Established in 1996, Hongyun Import & Export Co., Ltd. is a large state-owned corporation with 200 employees. It is located in the center of Tianjin, with convenient transportation access. It is engaged in the import and export of office equipments. The main products include laser printers, stylus printers, duplicating machines, group phones and office consumables, all of which are in line with international quality standards, are well received in a variety of markets both at home and abroad.

Based on well-equipped facilities and strict quality control throughout all stages of production, we are able to offer excellent products and services to our customers. And we have established stable and extensive cooperation with overseas customers from Thailand, Malaysia, Singapore and India, having constructed a widespread marketing network.

Our goal remains unchanged: Always providing our customers with products of high cost effectiveness and top quality services to guarantee total customer satisfaction.

We are confident that quality products with reasonable prices will bring you high economic benefits. And we would like to form successful business relationships with new clients around the world in the near future.

Have you got some ideas about how to write a corporate profile after studying the above sample? If so, you are expected to do a brief analysis of the above sample and write down the key points.

KEY POINTS HERE

_____
_____
_____
_____
_____
_____
_____
_____
_____
_____

Part II   Having a Clear Picture

I. Concept of Corporate Profile

A corporate profile is the basic information of a company or an organization, which can be seen on the newspaper, magazines, web pages and any other spreading materials. As a very important part of business activities, a corporate profile is intended for offering business information to the public, establishing a corporate image, and gaining more business opportunities.

II. Components of Corporate Profiles

The length of a corporate profile varies from organization to organization. The line of words or pattern on top of letter paper is in fact the simplest one. Sometimes they are specified to pages. Generally speaking, a corporate profile is composed of the following four sections.

1. An Overview

Several sentences are put at the beginning to introduce the major products and business direction of the company. For example:

Toshiba, a world leader in high technology, is active in three key domains: digital products (PCs and related equipment and peripherals, mobile phones, AV equipment), electronic devices & components (semiconductors, electron tubes, optoelectronic devices, LCDs, batteries, printed circuits boards, etc.) and infrastructure systems (industrial apparatus, power generating equipment, transportation equipment, social automation equipment, telecommunication systems, broadcasting systems, elevators, medical systems, etc.). Other businesses include consumer products, such as digital home products and home appliances.

2. A Brief Introduction to the Company's History

It is advisable to mention the establishment year and other vital-event years so as to impress customers. For example:

North-west Airlines began operations in 1926 and is American's oldest carrier with continuous name identification. It operates substantial domestic and international route networks and directly serves more than 750 cities in 120 countries on the continents of North America, Asia and Europe.

3. Present Situation

It deals with the essential part of the corporate profile, including the company's present scale, major products, managing range, achievements and corporate culture etc. For example:

Peking University Founder Corporation has dozens of joint ventures, domestic chain companies, and all-capital subsidiaries. There are more than a thousand agencies throughout the country. The products of the corporation include Fang Zheng Electronic Publishing System, Office Automation System, computer software and hardware products, biochemical products, mechanical and electronic products, etc. After a few years of pioneering efforts, the company has achieved an annual output value of over four hundred million Yuan in 1992.

4. Prospect

Finally, you need to use several sentences to describe the company's future development plan or potential prospect. For example:

We're determined to continuously improve our social and environmental performance. We work hard, together with our suppliers and independent restaurant franchisees, to strive toward a sustainable future — for our company and the communities in which we operate. From the beginning, we've been a company committed to doing the right thing. Today, our values continue to be the foundation for who we are, what we do, and how we operate.

III. Language Features of Corporate Profiles

As the business information from a corporate profile is to be brief, objective, exact and impressive, the language for a corporate profile must be modest, clear and trustable.

Therefore, it is required to avoid exaggeration and ambiguity.

Part III   Showing Your Talent Slightly

Now that you have had a clear picture of the components and language features of corporate profiles, you can fulfill the following situational task with the help of the Warm-up Case Study.

I. Situational Task

You work as a clerk in Public Relations Department, Tian Hai Fashion Co., Ltd. This morning, Mr. Zhang Ming, the manager asks you to draft a corporate profile of your company. The information is given below.

天海时装有限公司是一家迅速发展的企业。本公司自1998年投身于纺织和服装领域以来，一直追求卓越的品质和大众化价格。我们以优良的品质、诚信可靠和实惠的价格赢得了海内外客户的赞誉。

天海时装公司是全国最大的纺织品生产和出口基地之一。本公司出口各类羊毛、丝绸以及牛仔服装，质地极为柔滑。每件服装采用丝线、水晶珠、金属线等进行手工刺绣。

欢迎海内外客户前来洽谈业务，通力合作。

II. Do It Yourself

Tian Hai Fashion Co., Ltd.

_____
_____
_____
_____
_____
_____
_____
_____
_____
_____
_____
_____

Part IV   Opening the Treasure Box

I. Samples

Sample 1

> **Haier Group**
>
> Haier is the world's 4th largest white goods manufacturer and the most valuable brand in China. With 29 manufacturing plants, 8 comprehensive R&D centers, 19 overseas trading companies across the world and more than 50,000 global employees, Haier has developed into a giant multinational company. In 2008, Haier gained global revenue of RMB 119 billion.
>
> Thanks to 25 years of efforts, its reputation throughout the world has been heightened significantly. In 2008, the brand value of Haier amounted to impressive RMB 80.3 billion. Since 2002, Haier has topped the Most Valuable Brand tally for seven consecutive years. Nineteen Haier branded products, including refrigerator, air conditioner, washing machine, television, water heater, computer, mobile phone and home appliances integration, have been awarded as Chinese Famous Brand products. Haier refrigerator and washing machine are among the first group of Chinese World Famous Brand products awarded by the General Administration of Quality Supervision, Inspection and Quarantine of the P.R.C. In March 2008, Haier was selected as one of the "China's Top 10 Global Brands" by *Financial Times* for the second time. In June 2008, *Forbes* released the world's "600 Most Reputable Companies", of which Haier ranked the 13th and the 1st among Chinese companies. In July 2008, Haier ranked first in terms of overall leadership among Chinese mainland companies in *the Wall Street Journal* Asia's annual survey of "Asia's 200 Most Admired Companies". Haier has become an international brand, and its prestige is rising fast with its expansion into the international market.
>
> According to China Market Monitor, the most reliable market consultancy company in China, Haier held over 26.2% of China's household appliance market in 2008, thereby consolidating its market-leading position; and, in particular, its advantage is more noticeable in the high-end market, with an impressive market share of about 30%. It has been taking the lead among white goods brands. Moreover, Haier leads the world in intelligent home appliances integration, network household appliances, digitization, large scale integrated circuit and new materials. "Innovation driven" Haier has been committed to providing effective solutions to global consumers and achieving a win-win situation with them.

Haier's managerial models of "OEC", "market chain" and "individual-order combination" have been highly recognized worldwide. Its experience has also been introduced into case studies of many foreign educational institutes, including Harvard University, University of Southern California, International Institute for Management Development (IMD), the European Business College (in France) and Kobe University. Its "market chain" management practice has also been accepted into the EU case study library stock.

Haier has reached the fourth-year milestone in implementing its global branding strategy. It will continue to adhere to the corporate spirit of "creating resources and global reputation", and press ahead with the guiding principle of "combining individuals with orders; and acting fast to get success". By pushing forward the information process recreation, Haier will establish a user-centered process of information, a global network of logistics, fund and information flow, and a global leading brand that belongs to China.

Sample 2

McDonald's

McDonald's is the leading global food service retailer with more than 31,000 local restaurants serving more than 58 million people in 118 countries each day. More than 75% of McDonald's restaurants worldwide are owned and operated by independent local men and women. We serve the world some of its favorite foods — World Famous Fries, Big Mac, Quarter Pounder, Chicken McNuggets and Egg McMuffin.

Our rich history began with our founder, Ray Kroc. The strong foundation that he built continues today with McDonald's vision and the commitment of our talented executives to keep the shine on McDonald's Arches for years to come.

McDonald's success is built on a foundation of personal and professional integrity. Hundreds of millions of people around the world trust McDonald's. We earn that trust everyday by serving safe food, respecting our customers and employees and delivering outstanding Quality, Service, Cleanliness and Value (QSC&V). We build on this trust by being ethical, truthful and dependable.

We drive our business momentum by focusing on what matters most to customers. Our owner/operators, suppliers and employees work together to meet customer needs in uniquely McDonald's ways. The powerful combination of entrepreneurial spirit and systemwide alignment around our **Plan to Win** enables us to execute the best ideas with both large-scale efficiency and local flair.

Sample 3

China Petroleum & Chemical Corporation

China Petroleum & Chemical Corporation (hereinafter referred to as "Sinopec Corp.") is a listed company on domestic and international stock exchanges with integrated upstream, midstream and downstream operations, strong oil & petrochemical core businesses and a complete marketing network. The Company was incorporated on February 25th, 2000 by China Petrochemical Corporation (hereinafter referred to as "Sinopec Group") as the sole initiator, pursuant to the Company Law of the People's Republic of China. As of end 2007, the Company's total number of shares were 86.7 billion, of which 75.84% were held by Sinopec Group, 19.35% were shares listed overseas and 4.81% were domestic public shares.

Sinopec Corp. is one of the largest integrated energy and chemical companies in China. The scope of its business mainly covers oil and gas exploration and production, extraction, pipeline transmission and marketing, oil refining, production, marketing, storage and transportation of petrochemicals, chemical fibers, chemical fertilizers and other chemical products, import, export and import/export agency business of crude oil, natural gas, refined oil products, petrochemicals, chemicals, and other commodities and technologies, research, development and application of products (including gasoline, diesel and jet fuel, etc.) and major petrochemical products (including synthetic resin, synthetic fiber monomers and polymers, synthetic fiber, synthetic rubber, chemical fertilizer and petrochemical intermediates). It is also China's second largest crude oil producer.

Through years of reform, restructuring, strengthened management and innovation, the Company realized rapid development. Total assets increased by 40.8% and the shareholders' equity increased by 45.4%. The distributed dividend in the past three years amounted to RMB 37.7 billion, a relatively good reward for our shareholders. China Petrochemical Corporation with Sinopec Corp. as its core asset, ranked 16th in the 2008 Fortune 500 companies.

Sinopec Corp. has established a standardized structure of corporate governance. It has more than 80 subsidiaries and branches including wholly-owned, equity-holding and equity-sharing companies, engaging in oil and gas exploration and production, refining, chemicals, marketing, R&D and foreign trade. Business assets and principal markets are located in the east, south and middle part of China, where China's most developed and dynamic economy lies.

Sinopec Corp. carried out its social responsibilities and pushed forward harmonious development. We abided by the ten principles of the UN Global Compact by focusing on sustainable development, implementing HSE management systems and subsequently reported the Company's sustainability to stakeholders. The Company has actively engaged in the philanthropic events. In 2008, South China experienced a natural disaster caused by low-temperature sleet and frost. Furthermore, the Wenchuan earthquake shocked people across the globe. The company reacted quickly to organize and participate in rescue and relief efforts. The Company and employees donated money and materials worth RMB 300 million to the earthquake-stricken area.

As an endeavor to become a multinational energy and chemical company with fairly strong international competitiveness, Sinopec Corp. will seriously implement strategies of resource, market, integration and internationalization with more focus on innovation of science, technology and management expertise, as well as improvement of employees' quality.

Sample 4

DBS Group Holdings (DBS)

DBS Group Holdings (DBS) is one of the largest financial services groups in Asia. Headquartered in Singapore, DBS is a well-capitalized bank with "AA-" and "Aa1" credit ratings that are among the highest in the Asia-Pacific region.

DBS was established in 1968 as the development bank of Singapore. It was the catalyst to Singapore's economic development during the nation's early years of independence. Since then, DBS has transformed into a successful financial services institution, offering a comprehensive range of innovative products and solutions to meet its clients' needs. With operations in 16 markets, the bank has a regional network spanning more than 200 branches and over 1,000 ATMs across 50 cities.

As one of the leading banks in Asia, DBS also acknowledges the passion, commitment and can-do spirit in each of its 14,000 staff, representing over 30 nationalities. We are committed to empowering, educating and engaging our staff so as to build a high performance organization renowned for its good customer service and innovative business solutions.

DBS is a leading consumer bank in Singapore and Hong Kong, serving over 4 million and 1 million retail customers respectively. The bank has also been a key partner in spearheading and financing the growth of Singapore's small and medium-sized enterprises, or SMEs. In Hong Kong, DBS is a leading player in the SME banking space, with leading market shares in equipment and trade finance.

DBS is also a pioneer in the capital markets with extensive product origination and risk management capabilities. The bank was the first to launch Singapore's first real estate investment trust (Reit) in 2002 and is instrumental in meeting the growing demand of such funds in the region. It is also a well-regarded custodian for institutional investors and provider of wealth management products for individuals. A leader in treasury operations, DBS extends a broad range of capabilities in foreign exchange and derivatives, money market and securities trading to corporations and financial institutions.

Building on the strengths of its Singapore and Hong Kong businesses, DBS is steadily making its mark in the region. Greater China — comprising China, Hong Kong and Taiwan, is a key part of DBS' regional strategy. DBS is the first Singapore bank to incorporate in China, and has 40 distribution outlets and 5 DBS Treasures centers across the country.

In India, DBS has 10 branches across key cities like Mumbai and Delhi. DBS India also has a 37.5% stake in Cholamandalam DBS Finance Ltd, a non-bank financial institution. In Indonesia, DBS has a 99%-owned subsidiary, PT Bank DBS Indonesia, and is rapidly expanding its footprint across the country. It currently has a network of 40 branches spread across 11 cities.

II. Related Expressions

(1) Headquartered in Shanghai, China Merchants Bank is a...
招商银行总部设在上海，是一家……

(2) In 2004, this company was ranked 5th among...

在 2004 年，本公司位列……中的第五位。

(3) ... is a listed company on domestic and international stock exchanges.

……是一家在国内外证券交易所挂牌的上市公司。

(4) DBS is a pioneer in the capital markets with extensive product origination and risk management capabilities.

DBS 在资本市场居于领先地位，具备强大的产品研发和风险管理能力。

(5) thanks to 25 years of efforts　　经过 25 年的努力

(6) Established in 1970, this Company is a...

本公司成立于 1970 年，是一家……

(7) We are committed to providing quality products and excellent service for our customers.

我们承诺为客户提供优质的产品和服务。

(8) This Company carried out its social responsibilities and pushed forward harmonious development.

本公司认真履行社会责任，促进社会和谐发展。

(9) This Company is specialized in...　　本公司专门从事……

(10) Sinopec Corp. has established a standardized structure of corporate governance.

中国石化股份公司已经建立了标准的企业治理结构。

(11) McDonald's success is built on a foundation of...　　麦当劳的成功基于……

(12) It has been taking the lead among white goods brands.

该公司在白色家电行业居于领先地位。

(13) The company follows the principle of "Customer First" and offers high quality products combined with excellent services.

公司本着"顾客第一"的理念，为顾客提供优质的产品和服务。

(14) We have a powerful expert team engaging in designing the most fashionable colors and styles.

我们拥有实力雄厚的专家组，专门从事最时髦的颜色和款式的设计。

(15) Our R&D team turns out one product every three weeks to keep up with the latest market trends. We are confident we can meet your OEM/ODM requirements.

为紧跟市场趋势，我们的研发团队每三个星期推出一款新产品。我们自信能够达到你方的 OEM/ODM 要求。

III. Functional Sentences

(1) For three consecutive years since 1990, our company has been listed as one of the

top 30 enterprises among China's 500 largest foreign trade companies in import-export volumes.

自1990年起，公司已连续三年在中国进出口额最大的500家外贸企业中进入前30位。

(2) This Company has a long history, rich experience and reliable reputation.

本公司历史悠久，经验丰富，信誉可靠。

(3) We are New England's largest antique and fine arts auction house with some of the country's most knowledgeable professional on staff.

我们是新英格兰最大的古玩艺术拍卖行，拥有全国最内行的行家。

(4) We start with impeccable quality to provide exceptional value. Then we add a special personal touch.

我们为您提供超值的服务，是从确保产品完美的品质开始的，其次是我们特有的人性化服务。

(5) Our products rank first among similar products.

我们的产品居同类产品之魁首。

(6) Its unique design makes its "Xinxing" Brand jacket sell as far as to more than 30 countries and regions in the world, all well received by the broad users at home and abroad.

其独特的设计使其"新星"牌夹克产品远销世界30多个国家和地区，深受广大用户的欢迎。

(7) Time Warner Inc., created in 1990, is one of the largest media and entertainment corporations in the world.

时代华纳公司成立于1990年，是世界上最大的传媒和娱乐公司之一。

(8) Tianjin World Economy Trade and Exhibition Center is a first class modern comprehensive exhibition and trade center jointly operated by China, Germany and Japan. It is the most ideal place for various kinds of international exhibitions, trade fairs and conventions.

天津国际经济贸易展览中心是由中国、德国和日本合资经营的综合性现代化大型国际展览与经济贸易中心，是举办各种规模和类型的国际展览会、博览会及国际会议的理想场所。

(9) The factory can produce various new types of buttons in thousands of different designs for coats, suits, fashions, shirts and sweaters.

该厂能生产大衣、西装、时装、衬衣、毛衣等不同类型服装用的上千花色品种的纽扣，产品规格齐全、品种繁多、造型新颖。

(10) Through the leading manufacture, research and development, Samsung has become

one of the world's fastest-growing groups.

由于研发、制造方面的领先优势，三星集团已成为世界上增长速度最快的集团之一。

(11) After just a few years of pioneering efforts, the company has achieved an annual output value of over 400 million dollars in 2003.

经过几年的努力，公司 2003 年的产值已超过 4 亿美元。

(12) Friends and business partners all over the world are welcome to establish business ties with us on the basis of equality and mutual benefit so that they can enjoy sincere cooperation and joint development with us.

我们热忱欢迎世界各地工商界朋友，在平等互利原则下，与我们建立业务联系，真诚合作、共同发展。

(13) The company boasts tremendous technological strength with well-qualified management and staff.

本公司拥有雄厚的技术力量和高素质的管理人员和员工。

(14) We have been in the silk garment trade for 35 years. Our products find a ready market in over 50 countries and regions.

我们厂生产的丝绸衬衣已有 35 年的悠久历史，产品大量销往 50 多个国家和地区。

(15) Not only are we at the forefront of electronics, but we've received worldwide recognition for our advances in chemicals and engineering as well.

我们不仅处于电子技术的前沿，而且在化工和工程技术方面取得的进展也同样得到世界范围的认可。

(16) Haier has owned a wide range of product groups of 69 categories with over 10800 specifications including white household appliance, black household appliance, and rice kernel household appliance.

海尔目前已拥有包括白色家电、黑色家电、米色家电在内的 69 大门类 10800 个规格品种的产品群。

(17) In 2012, this Group was listed as the 114th of the world top 500 enterprises.

2012 年，本集团在世界企业 500 强中名列第 114 位。

(18) Wal-Mart was founded in 1962, with the opening of the first Wal-Mart discount store in Rogers, Arkansas.

沃尔玛公司成立于 1962 年，在阿肯色州罗杰斯城设立了第一家沃尔玛平价店。

(19) We are known around the world as the company that helps our customers save more money so they can live better.

我们公司以"为顾客省钱从而使他们生活更好"而著称于世。

(20) At the core of every one of our business philosophy and corporate culture is the basic value of respect — for the customers, associates and suppliers.

在我们所有的经营理念和企业文化中,尊重顾客、员工和供应商是核心价值观。

Part V　Displaying Your Prowess Fully

I. Draft a corporate profile for Broadway Autos according to the information given below in Chinese.

百老汇汽车公司（Broadway Autos）简介

百老汇汽车公司是设在俄勒冈州波特兰市（Portland, Oregon）的百老汇国际公司（Broadway International Inc.）的子公司。该公司生产并销售两种电瓶驱动的汽车：短程送货车和单人座残疾人车。车身在百老汇汽车公司所属的工厂里生产，但是其他部件，包括电动机、蓄电池组和车轮都是外购的，备有两个月的库存，并在该厂组装。多年来，百老汇与其他供货商建立了良好的关系，其中大部分供货商已与之合作多年。

II. Translate the following corporate profile of Fuji-Xerox into Chinese.

Fuji-Xerox is one of the most enduring and reportedly successful alliances between two companies from different countries. Established in 1962, Fuji-Xerox today is structured as a 50/50 joint venture between the Xerox Group, the US maker of photocopiers, and Fuji Photo Film, Japan's largest manufacturer of film products. With sales of close to $10 billion, Fuji-Xerox provides Xerox with over 20 percent of its worldwide revenues. A prime motivation to establish the joint venture was the Japanese government's refusal in the early 1960s to allow foreign companies to set up wholly owned subsidiaries in Japan. The joint venture was conceived as a marketing organization to sell xerographic products that would be manufactured by Fuji Photo under license from Xerox. However, when the Japanese government refused to approve the establishment of a joint venture intended solely as a sales company, the joint venture agreement was revised to give Fuji-Xerox manufacturing rights.

III. Draft a corporate profile of Beijing Quanjude Roast Duck Restaurant according to the information given below in Chinese.

北京全聚德烤鸭店简介

全聚德创建于1864年，距今已有150多年历史，是中外闻名的老字号风味饭庄。北京全聚德烤鸭店主要经营挂炉烤鸭和山东风味菜肴，以及独具风味的"全鸭席"。它具有雄厚的烹饪技术力量，拥有一大批著名的烹饪高手。

北京全聚德烤鸭店座落在北京前门西大街。这幢七层大楼建于1979年，总建筑面积15000平方米，共有大小餐厅40余间，可同时接待2000位宾客，是目前中国，也是世界上专营烤鸭的最大饭庄。餐厅环境优雅、舒适、富丽堂皇。

北京全聚德烤鸭店全体员工，热忱欢迎中外宾客前来品尝全聚德名优烤鸭，并以饱满的热情、优雅的环境竭诚为您服务。

IV. Translate the following corporate profile of Bank of China into Chinese.

Bank of China, or Bank of China Limited in full, is one of China's four state-owned commercial banks. Its businesses cover commercial banking, investment banking and insurance. Members of the group include BOC Hong Kong, BOC International, BOCG Insurance and other financial institutions. The Bank provides a comprehensive range of high-quality financial services to individual and corporate customers as well as financial institutions worldwide. In terms of tier one capital, it ranked 10th among the world's top 1000 banks by *The Banker* magazine in 2008.

The Bank is mainly engaged in commercial banking, including corporate and retail banking business and financial institutions banking. Corporate banking is built upon credit products, to provide customers with personalized and innovative financial services. Retail banking serves the financial needs of the Bank's individual customers, focusing on providing them with services in terms of bank credit cards. Financial institution banking refers to services offered to banks, securities brokerages, fund companies and insurance companies worldwide ranging from foreign exchange, funds clearing, inter-bank lending/borrowing, custodian services, etc.

V. Translate the following corporate profile of BodyWave (Ningbo) Cosmetics Co., Ltd. into Chinese.

BodyWave (Ningbo) Cosmetics Co., Ltd. is a subsidiary established in China in 2003 by American BodyWave Shareholding Co., Ltd., with the registered capital of US$3.06 million and the independent status of a legal person. It is a professional import & export company approved by competent foreign trade and economic cooperation authorities. It is located in central Ningbo City, with an office area of 2000 square meters and a staff number of over 30, including 8 technicians. It has 2 cooperative factories and maintains permanent cooperation with some other professional factories within and around Zhejiang Province. Therefore, it boasts stable sources of goods and a professional service team.

Its imports cover top-quality cosmetics, raw material for cosmetics and beautification equipment, the major of which are imported from the United States, with the annual import volume amounting to more than US$10 million. Its exports cover articles for women and infants, such as cosmetics, top-quality ornaments, textile and small articles, the major of which are exported to the United States, Europe, Middle East, South America and Japan.

With its organizational culture of "care, cause and share" and its service philosophy of "reputation and customer priority", BodyWave (Ningbo) Cosmetics Co., Ltd. would like to cooperate with its partners both at home and abroad to create a more prosperous future.

Instruction

Part I Warm-up Case Study

Fasten your belt! You can begin an exciting journey towards learning to write an instruction efficiently by reading the following sample instruction. While studying the sample, you need to discuss its function, components, types and writing style. Finally, you are expected to explore the writing techniques on drafting an instruction in a professional way. Now let's come to the following sample.

Dumpling Machine (Model GCE-4)

GCE-4 dumpling machine, latest designed food processing machine can make not only meat or vegetable-meat dumplings, but also sweet-filling fried ones, suitable for restaurants, dumpling restaurants and canteens.

Small in size, reasonable in structure, easy in operation, convenient for cleaning, strong and long lasting in use, reliable in sanitation, the machine can mix up flour and finings at will, and make dumplings with thin coverings and full filling, matching well with hand-made dumplings both in shape and in flavor.

Technical Specifications:

Output: 6000 dumplings/hour

Standard: 7–8 dumplings/50g

Electric motor: JO22-6 1.1 Watt, 930 rotations/minutes, three-phase 380 volts/220volts

Exterior measurements (length × breadth × height): 740 × 360 × 1020 (mm)

Total weight: 170kg

Have you got some ideas about how to write an instruction after studying the above sample? If so, you are expected to do a brief analysis of the above sample and write down the key points.

KEY POINTS HERE

_____
_____
_____
_____
_____
_____
_____

Part II Having a Clear Picture

I. Concept of Instruction

Instructions are common in the workplace and people's daily life. They are used to transmit the function, characteristic, and directions for use of products. By means of instructions, manufacturers explain to users how to operate a device or use a product. User-friendly and effective instructions can result in greater consumer confidence in the product. This certainly helps to improve the image of the manufacturer.

II. Components of Instructions

Most instructions are stated in the light of process analysis and put in order step by step. Generally speaking, a copy of instruction is made up of four parts: introduction, list of steps, explanation of steps and conclusion.

1. Introduction

The introduction should define the process and name of the products to be made. It explains what materials, equipment, tools and skills are needed for the task.

2. List of Steps

The list of steps contains every step and the order of steps must be correct and logical. Only a brief explanation is required.

3. Explanation of Steps

The explanation of steps is necessary in instructions. Because it provides some useful information on how to use something or how something should be done. Readers will easily perform on the goods with the explanation of steps. In addition, it must be written in detail.

4. Conclusion

Repeating the importance of some useful information in the instruction. And it is also necessary to make further explanation of something that should be done while using.

III. Types of Instructions

According to the functions of an instruction, they can be classified into three types: sales specifications, usage directions and maintenance directions. A detailed study will be given to the first two types of specifications.

1. Sales Instruction

A sales instruction is to promote the manufacturer's products and services. It deals with the brand, function, technical data and unique features of the products. In addition, a brief introduction to manufacturers and distributors can be given in a sales instruction. People can see sales instructions when they are visiting a trade fair.

2. Usage Directions

A usage direction is to show the customers how to use the products by focusing on the function, performance, operation and precautions of the products. Effective usage directions are complete and precise. They give all the necessary steps and details so that the users can get the job done without unreasonable guesswork.

3. Maintenance Directions

A maintenance direction is mostly prepared for maintenance technicians. It is to give a complete account of the structure, features, functions, failure cause and troubleshooting procedures of the products. Maintenance directions are closely related to mechanical products, instruments and electronic products.

IV. Language Features of Instructions

Instructions are to show the customers how to use the product exactly and properly. Therefore, the language should be short and simple, clear and exact, with precision and logic, so that the users can easily understand the function and directions for use as well as the way of protection. It is better to use passive voice in drafting an instruction when explaining the function of products.

Part III Showing Your Talent Slightly

Now that you have had a clear picture of the components and language features of an instruction, you can fulfill the following situational task with the help of the Warm-up Case Study.

I. Situational Task

You work as an office clerk in Sales Department, ABC Co., Ltd. This morning, Miss Zhang Ling, the manager asks you to draft an instruction for Poly Clean. The information is given below.

保洁丽 (Poly Clean)

保洁丽配方独特，能迅速清除玻璃、窗户及其他硬物表面的污垢和尘迹，方便快捷。用后不留痕迹，令物件光洁明亮。尤其适用于清洁玻璃、窗户、汽车玻璃、不锈钢、塑料、瓷器及人造革表面等。

使用方法：拧开瓶嘴，将保洁丽喷于需要清洁的物件上，然后用清洁的纸巾或干布抹拭。

注意事项：若不慎此液沾眼，请立即用清水冲洗。如误饮本清洁剂，请立即饮用大量清水并就医诊治。请勿用于漆面。

II. Do It Yourself

POLY CLEAN

_____
_____
_____
_____
_____
_____
_____
_____
_____
_____
_____
_____
_____
_____
_____

Part IV Opening the Treasure Box

I. Samples

Sample 1 A Sales Instruction for Angel Brand String Instruments

Angel Brand String Instruments

The manufacturer of "Angel" Brand String Instruments has long been engaged in this occupation, thus having acquired rich experience.

Made of selected timber, equipped with exquisite accessories and finished with fine workmanship, "Angel" Brand String Instruments are elegant in appearance and brilliant in varnish. They are warmly received by people of all kinds both at home and abroad including professional musicians, students and music beginners for their graceful tune, great volume and harmonious sound.

"Angel" Brand String Instruments cover a wide range of items for cellos, violins, basses, guitars and ukuleles in all specifications. Also available are hornpipes, mouth organs, metronomes. In addition to normal trading, we also welcome all flexible dealings such as processing with supplied materials, samples and brands.

All are welcome to approach China National Light Industrial Products Import and Export Corporation, Jiangsu Branch.

Sample 2 Usage Directions for Kenwood Dynamic Microphone MC-550

Kenwood Dynamic Microphone MC-550 Instruction Manual

Main Features

- The magnet is made from neodymium so that high level and high quality sound is produced.
- The unit employs a double dome diaphragm in order to achieve a well-balanced sound quality from the lower range to the upper range.
- A light duty CCAW (aluminum wire) is employed for the voice coil in order to achieve a crystal clear sound quality.
- A reliable Canon brand connector is employed.

Operating Instructions

• Insert the microphone plug into the microphone terminal.

• Flip the microphone switch to the "ON" position and adjust the volume with the volume control knob on the amplifier.

• When handling the microphone to somebody else or when finish using, flip the microphone switch to the "OFF" position.

Handling Precautions

• If the microphone head is covered by hand or the microphone is approached to the speaker, a howling sound may be generated. This phenomenon of howling is caused by the microphone picking up the sound output from the speaker. To prevent this, first decrease the volume, then place the microphone so that it is not pointed to the speaker and there is a sufficient distance between the microphone and the speaker.

• The microphone is sensitive equipment. Do not drop, hit it or apply strong shock to it.

• Do not store the microphone in a place with high temperature or humidity.

Pointer for Proper Use of Microphone

The optimum distance between the microphone and the mouth is from 5 to 10 centimeters. If the microphone is too close to the mouth, the sound may be unclear with too much enhanced base (proximity effect) or may be uncomfortable to ears with pop noise generated every time when the singer breathes in and out.

Sample 3 A Sales Instruction for MORNFLAKE

MORNFLAKE

Selected Oatflakes with High Quality

Originated from England, the producer of raw materials is Morning Food Co., Ltd., founded in 1675. Monde Selection, international Institute for Quality Selection, awarded it International High Quality Trophy several times for its quality, which can be regarded as the guarantee of the quality. No preservative and other additive have been added into this product.

Delicious Nutrition for Your Family

Mornflake Oatmeal is made from well-chosen oats in northern Britain so as to guarantee that you and your family members will enjoy the delicate and full-bodied flavor of this light and smooth oatmeal. You can also try your own unique flavor with this product by adding different ingredients that you prefer.

Nutrition Information

Free from milk, sugar and salt

Main Nutrition	Content per 100g
Energy	1500kg
Protein	12.0g
Carbohydrate	60.0g
Fat	7.5g
Dietary Fibre	4.0g
Sodium	30.0g

Recipe for Instant Drinking

Mix 3–4 tablespoons of oats with some boiling water or milk, and stir thoroughly.

Recipe for Microwave–oven Cooking

Put 3–4 tablespoons of oats into the microwave-oven container with 1.5 cup of water or milk. Boil at high temperature for 90 seconds. Light food preferred, please add more water; featured food preferred, please mix any ingredients preferred.

Sample 4 A Usage Direction for Medicine

Tabellae Qingchunbao

(Anti-aging Tablets)

Name of Product Anti-Aging Tablet

Property

The tablets have sugar coatings. When the coatings are removed, they appear brown with light sweet and bitter taste.

Main Ingredients

Radix Ginseng, Radix Asparagi, Radix Rehmanniae.

Effects and Indication

(1) Increase mental capacity, soothe nerves and strengthen vigor of thinking;

(2) Contribute to anti-fatigue, maintain unflagging strength and improve suitability to ill natural environment;

(3) Enhance faculties of nonspecific immunity and build up resistance to diseases;

(4) Strengthen heart functions, improve nourishment to cardiac muscles, prevent or reduce coronary heart diseases.

Notes

The tablets are scientifically and carefully prepared with traditional Chinese herbs on the basis of the prescription of Yongle Imperial Hospital of the Ming Dynasty. No hormone. No undesirable side effects have been observed with constant taking of the tablets.

Administration and Dosage

3–5 tablets should be orally taken each time, two times a day.

Specifications

Each tablet weighs 0.3 gram.

Ratification Document No. Guo Yao Zhun Zi B20021021

Storage

To be stored in an airtight container and kept in a cool, dark and dry place. Away from light.

Packaging   80 tablets per bottle.

Validity   Two years.

II. Related Expressions

(1) ... has been specially formulated for...　　……特别为……配制

(2) ... contains special conditioners to protect and care furniture. It will remove fingerprints, smudges and dirt.

……含有保护家具的特效调节剂，能有效擦去手印、污渍和灰尘。

(3) The usual dosage is... capsule daily or consult a physician; children over... years old may use adult dosage or consult a physician; children under age of... may take... capsule daily.

成人每日……粒，或遵医嘱；……岁以上儿童，按成人剂量，或遵医嘱；……岁以下儿童，每日……粒。

(4) In case of a reaction during the application such as intense stinging, rash or a burning sensation on the scalp, rinse immediately with lukewarm water.

如在使用本产品过程中，有强烈刺激感、红肿或灼痛现象发生，请立即用温水冲洗干净。

(5) Products of this kind are characterized by... They are widely used in...
该产品具有……特点，广泛应用于……

(6) These silk blouses are made of pure silk of the finest quality. They are moderately priced, of excellent craftsmanship and unique in design.
这些女士衬衣采用上等纯丝制成，价格公道，工艺精湛，设计独特。

(7) The product is allowed to leave the factory only after strict examination of its quality.
本产品经过严格的质量检查后出厂。

(8) The product can be used by men and women of all ages with no side or toxic effects.
本产品适用于男女老幼，无任何毒副作用。

(9) The essence can supplement moisture in time and help to regenerate cells.
这种精华液能及时为你的皮肤补充水分，促进细胞再生。

(10) It prevents and slows down excessive production of melanin.
本品能防止和延缓黑色素的过旺分泌。

(11) It soothes out fine wrinkles and diminishes signs of fatigue, evens out the skin tone of the face.
本品有效抚平细纹，舒缓皮肤疲劳，平衡肤色。

(12) Smooth emulsion over cleansed face with a circle motion.
洁面后，取适量乳液从面部中间往四周涂抹。

(13) Push the trimmer slide key upwards until it is fixed, then run the shaver.
将修剪滑面刀片按键推上去，待安装到位后开始剃须。

(14) For its structure and refined process, false use would result in outer net guard damage.
由于剃须刀结构精细复杂，使用时要谨慎细心，否则会损坏外部网罩。

(15) To clean the shaver, press down the blame frame, release button to dissemble the blade frame.
清洁剃须刀时，按住刀锋框架，按下按钮将刀锋框架拆下来。

III. Functional Sentences

(1) Protein and fat are essential nutrients that provide the majority of energy in cat food.
蛋白质和脂肪是猫粮中的必要营养素，也是猫粮中主要的能量来源。

(2) Granisetron is a potent and highly selective 5-hydroxytryptamine (5-HT 3) receptor antagonist with antiemetic activity.
凯特瑞是一种强效且具有高度选择性的 5- 羟色胺（5-HT3）受体对抗剂，具抗呕吐作用。

(3) Put several drops of product per liter of water to rinse the fruit or vegetables. Leave the fruit or vegetables in the rinsing water for 5 minutes. Before eating, rinse them with clean water.

清洗蔬菜瓜果时，每公升水加入本品数滴，浸泡5分钟后，用清水冲洗即可食用。

(4) Due to its unique formulation, Hazeline Snow is suitable for the skin of children and adults.

夏士莲雪花膏配方独特，适合儿童和成年人的皮肤。

(5) To obtain the best performance and ensure years of trouble-free use, please read this instruction manual carefully.

请仔细阅读说明书，以便发挥其最佳性能，经久耐用，不出故障。

(6) Carpets made in Xinjiang are famous for their novel designs and elegant colors. They are loved by everyone who sees them.

新疆生产的地毯图案新颖，色彩雅致，人见人爱。

(7) Should you encounter some problems during the installation or use of this computer, please refer to this troubleshooting guide prior to calling the helpdesk. Look up the problem in the left column and then check the suggestions in the right column.

当您在安装或使用本计算机时，如遇到问题，在打电话给客户服务部之前，请先参考本疑难排解之说明。请先在左栏中寻找您遇到的问题，然后在右栏中查看建议的解决方法。

(8) Perform a skin sensitivity test of 48 hours before using this product, even if you have already previously used a hair colorant of this or any other brand.

即使您原来用过此品牌或其他品牌的染发剂，在使用此产品之前，仍需进行皮肤敏感性测试达48小时之久。

(9) Store away from light in a cool place after dissolving a tablet.

药片溶解后，溶液应置于阴凉避光处保存。

(10) The products can be installed in several types such as cabinet, vertical racks, horizontal racks, ground placement and installed with other kinds of power supply cabinet according to user's requirements.

本产品可根据用户需要采用柜式、立架式、卧式、地面摆放及与其他电源柜内置式使用等各种形式。

(11) Special function on this model is touch-screen, TV-out and multi-games.

这种型号的特殊功能是触摸屏、电视输出和同时进行的多场游戏。

(12) It can play audio and video files in any format, without convert tool. Stable quality and stylish body.

可以播放任何格式的音频和视频文件，不需要转换工具。质量稳定，外形时尚。

(13) It is small in size and convenient to carry; besides, it is easy to operate.

体积小，携带方便，操作简单。

(14) It comes in four/a wide range of colors.

有四种/多种颜色。

(15) It is specially designed for extracting juice from fruit and vegetables.

专门为榨取水果和蔬菜的汁而设计的。

(16) The product will be delivered within three days and has a 24-month guarantee.

本产品保证期为24个月，3天内交货。

(17) We provide free 24-hour delivery and 30-day money-back guarantee.

我们提供24小时免费送货上门，30天退款保证。

(18) This bike is suitable for children aged 10–16.

这种自行车适合10～16岁的儿童。

(19) It has been proved that Lvyuan Taigan is able to produce certain medical effects, namely, to allay internal heat and fever, to reduce hypertension, to regulate and strengthen bodily functions, to relieve halitosis and to dispel the effects of alcohol.

绿源苔干具有清热降压、通经脉、壮筋骨、去口臭、解酒毒的功效。

Part V Displaying Your Prowess Fully

I. Draft an instruction for Salt Crackers according to the hints given below in Chinese.

咸味饼干介绍

我们的咸味饼干采用优质的原料，结合多重精细的制作过程，创造出了极为独特的口味，一定会成为您休闲时间的最佳食品。

配料：小麦，食用油，奶油，鸡蛋，盐

储藏方法：请存于阴凉干燥处

保质期：12个月

II. Draft an instruction for an electric kettle according to the hints given below in Chinese.

升华牌电热水壶

介绍：

本厂生产的电热水壶是最新流行的快速煮沸开水及饮料的家用电器产品，适用于家庭及工作单位。其结构合理，工艺先进，并具有热效率高、耗电量少、性能可靠、安全卫生等优点，是您的理想选择。

注意事项：

(1) 本产品启用前，必须复核电源线路容量，方可使用。

(2) 切勿将插座、插头浸水或溅湿，防止漏电，严禁将壶体浸入水中。

(3) 严禁少水或无水使用，以免损坏电热管。

(4) 水沸时注意外溢，防止漏电。

(5) 本产品只限于电热方式煮水，不得启用其他方式煮水。

(6) 为确保安全，禁止不接地使用。

III. Fill in the blanks to complete the following sales instruction for rotary oven by translating the given Chinese in the brackets into English.

CKFZ-70Y Rotary Oven

Uses and Features

The CKFZ-70Y Rotary Oven is ___(1)___ (高度专用性和可靠性的炊事设备) designed and made specially for roasting poultry and meat delicacies. ___(2)___ (广泛适用于餐厅、宾馆、零售店、酒吧、俱乐部、家庭及任何需要制作精美烧烤食品的场所).

___(3)___ (本烤炉提供的生产容量为一次可烤制 30 只仔鸡或者各种排骨、肉类 12 ~ 15 千克). It is complete with accessories including six stainless steel and six metal grills.

Fitted with glass doors in its front and in its back, and highly effectively heating system inside the oven, the CKFZ-70Y Rotary Oven is easy to operate. And ___(4)___ (操作者可清楚地观察烹调的全过程) which adds spice to the delicious food. The whole interior of the Rotary Oven is made of high-quality stainless steel. ___(5)___ (下端的加热器表面选用了洁净的陶瓷材料，既卫生又美观).

___(6)___ (炉温可随意调整，自动控制). The intensity of the heat can be set at will.

Parameters and Specifications

Power source three-phase four-wire 380V/220V50Hz

Electrocaloric power 6.6kw

Controllable temperature 20℃ –300℃

Power of driving motor 0.06kw

Dimensions of boy (length × depth × height) 104 × 85 × 171cm

IV. Draft an instruction for Electric Mosquito Killer according to the hints given below in Chinese.

1. 产品用途：杀灭蚊虫新产品；

2. 产品特点：三层金属网构成，快速灭蚊、无味、无污染，室内外皆可使用；

3. 使用方法：装两节 AAA 电池，紧握拍子，按下拍子电源按钮，指示红灯亮。

灭蚊蝇时，确保一直按下拍子电源按钮，一旦蚊虫身体靠近内网，蚊虫就会被电击且立刻被杀死；

4. 注意事项：通电时，请勿用手触碰电蚊拍外网、请勿水洗、请勿在有易燃气体或液体的地方使用。

V. Draft an instruction for Changcheng Dry Red Wine according to the hints given below in Chinese.

本产品是精选中国著名葡萄产区沙城地区（怀涿盆地）长城公司葡萄园的国际酿酒名种葡萄赤霞珠（Cabernet Sauvignon）为原料，严格按照国际葡萄酒 AOC（产地命名酒）标准，采用法国陈酿酒专用酵母橡皮桶发酵，陈酿八年以上等先进工艺精酿而成的鉴赏型高档红葡萄酒。该葡萄酒呈棕红色，酒体澄清，酒香沉馥优雅，橡木香味细腻，酒体丰满，展现了干红葡萄酒独特风味。

Sales Letter

Part I Warm-up Case Study

Fasten your belt! You can begin an exciting journey towards learning to write a sales letter efficiently by reading the following sample sales letter. While studying the sample, you need to discuss its function, components, types and writing style. Finally, you are expected to explore the writing techniques on drafting a sales letter in a professional way. Now let's come to the following sample.

Dear Customer,

Have you ever felt anything both soft and strong?

Believe it or not, this enclosed small sample of leather used in our new Gold Star leather bags will offer you such a feeling.

Give a touch to the sample and you will find that the leather our manufacturer is going to use is just as soft as a piece of cloud. But top quality leather is only one feather of the new Gold Star line, and style is another. Consequently it has won this year's First National Award for its gentleness and elegance. Wherever you go with it, you may be sure that your Gold Star leather bag will draw attention (perhaps even envy) from your companions.

In addition, the Gold Star leather bag has plenty of room for different items, and it even has a secret compartment for heaven-knows-what. For your information, the leather bags are designed in a variety of colors available in camel, white, navy blue, brown and black.

> As a result of the recognition, it is not surprising that this fashion line of our leather bags is being sold by all the top department stores in our country and has also been accepted by many dealers from European markets.
>
> Complete the order form and return it right now. We trust that your trial order may convince you that this $85 leather bag is of excellent value. You will receive a bottle of foam cream (leather clean) as a gift if you let us have your preference by sending the completed order form before May 1.
>
> Sincerely yours,
Bob Smith

Have you got some ideas about how to write a sales letter after studying the above sample letter? If so, you are expected to do a brief analysis of the above sample and write down the key points.

KEY POINTS HERE

_____
_____
_____
_____
_____
_____
_____

Part II Having a Clear Picture

I. Concept of Sales Letter

A sales letter is to expand business, to persuade the reader (namely the buyer) to buy what the sellers are able to supply (goods and services). This kind of writing is the most effective and least expensive way to reach potential buyers.

II. Components of Sales Letters

The modern trend in sales letter writing is towards making the letters more personal. A good sales letter writer tries to represent the offer from the point of view of the buyer, not the seller. Usually a sales message is usually made up of four parts:

1. Opening (to arouse readers' attention)

A sales letter must attract the attention of the targeted readers. Unless it gains attention early, the sales letter is most likely to be ignored. In order to catch the readers' attention, a writer may begin his sales message by stating a problem, asking a rhetorical question, or promising something of benefit, etc. The following examples are from some effective sales messages:

Our city spends more for alcohol than for education!

What if the boss came to your desk and said, "We are going to increase production by 13 percent this week"?

Why not enjoy the colorful spring by joining our tourist group after a busy winter?

"The common cold causes other illnesses, but a bottle of COLD medicine at hand helps you solve your problem completely," says a prominent doctor from the National Medical Research Center.

2. Appeal Description (to create interest and desire)

When you have successfully arrested your readers' attention, you should proceed to create interest and desire. The critical point is to make your goods or services attractive and unique. That is to say, a writer must study the product or service and then choose the right appeal. Appeals mean the strategies you use to present a product or service to your readers. Appeals can be divided into two broad categories: emotional and rational. In emotional appeals, your persuasive efforts are directed to how people feel, taste, smell, hear, and see. In rational appeals, your persuasive efforts are directed to reason — the thinking mind. Such appeals include strategies based on saving money, making money, doing a better job, or getting better use from a product.

In any given case, many appeals are available to you. The choice depends on the product or service, and on your readers. Such products as perfume, candy, and fine food lend themselves to emotional appeals. On the other hand, such products as automobile tires, tools and industrial equipment are best sold through rational appeals. Sometimes we can use both emotional and rational appeals.

3. Specific Explanation (to convince readers)

Once you have obtained your readers' attention and developed it into interest and desire, you proceed to point out and stress all the benefits that your product and service can offer. You need to show how your products or service will make your reader's job easier, increase his status, make personal life more pleasant, and so on. The following two examples are good illustrations.

After a few minutes' instructions, your office workers, too, can begin making perfect copies in six seconds or less; and if you need ten such copies a day, the $500 you spend for the machine can be saved in three months.

Within one year of your purchase of the computer, we will take care of fixing, repairing, or even replacing it if there is anything wrong.

4. Closing (to motivate readers' action)

In this part, you usually tell your readers how to obtain the product or service. You may request your reader to provide personal information on an enclosed card, to come to your showroom for a demonstration, or to authorize a home sales visit. And you can offer incentives that will make your reader responsive. For example, you might send a gift, stress limited availability, offer a special discount for a limited period of time, or suggest a deferred payment plan. The following are two good examples.

Fill in the enclosed order blank and mail it by January 1, and we'll ship you 1000 free sheets of the specially treated copy paper along with the machine.

Why wait? Come and buy the machine right now as a special discount of 15% will be offered only for a month.

III. Types of Sales Letters

There are different methods to classify sales letters. In terms of their forms, sales letters can be divided into two types: solicited sales letters and unsolicited sales letters.

1. Solicited Sales Letters

A solicited sales letter is a reply to a letter of inquiry by a customer in terms of the products and services. It is to retain or regain the customer by highlighting the writer's products and services.

2. Unsolicited Sales Letters

An unsolicited sales letter is a promotional letter to present the writer's products and services to a potential customer even if the writer has not received a letter of inquiry by the potential customer. It is written to attract new customers by presenting the writer's products and services.

IV. Tips for Sales Letter Writing

Sales letters are widely used now in business practice, so it is very necessary to write an effective sales letter. In order to successfully persuade the potential customer, the sales letter must be greatly characteristic and attractive.

1. In Language

(1) Be brief, short and easy to understand. People will not read a long and complicated

sales letter.

(2) Be direct. The content of the letter simply tells the function of the products and needs of the customer.

(3) Be practical and sensible. Try not to talk big but be reasonable.

(4) Be innovative. Try to use new, forceful words to introduce your products or services.

(5) Be considerate. Adopt you-attitude. Create an atmosphere of intimate personal relationship.

2. In Appearance

Sales letters are one of the most creative letters in business communication. Besides the attractiveness of the language and content, they are better delicately designed with a new style. The key words may be underlined, color-changed or made with some other attractive change.

Part III Showing Your Talent Slightly

Now that you have had a clear picture of the components and language features of sales letters, you can fulfill the following situational task with the help of the Warm-up Case Study.

I. Situational Task

You work as a clerk in Sales Department, ABC Co., Ltd. This morning, Mr. Li Wei, the department head asks you to draft a sales letter about your products. The information is given below.

ABC公司新推出一款拼写&语法软件包（SPELLGRAM software package），该软件包能检查出70,000多英文单词的拼写错误，还能纠正常见的英语词、句法、标点错误。该软件需要128兆的储存配置，适用于检查英国英语和美国英语文档。该款软件具备实用、灵活和便捷的特点。

II. Do It Yourself

_____
_____
_____
_____
_____
_____

Part IV Opening the Treasure Box

I. Samples

Sample 1 A Solicited Sales Letter for Office Furniture

Dear Mr. John,

We thank you for your inquiry about our newly designed office furniture. It is a great pleasure to serve you again.

The items you inquired in your letter are selling extremely well in our area. They are very easy to use, convenient for filing documents, and taking much less space than previous ones. In addition, they are at least 25% lower in cost compared with our previous ones and those of our competitors.

Your order can be delivered to your central warehouse in Los Angeles within 30 working days after we receive it. And a discount of 10 percent on the total value is possible if payment is made within 15 days of delivery.

Please order without delay since our popular products may well be out of stock soon. We are looking forward to working on your order again.

Yours sincerely,
Adam Smith

Sample 2 A Solicited Sales Letter for Anesthesia Machine

Dear Dr. Arnold,

The enclosed reports from our previous customers will, we are sure, give you the information requested in your letter dated September 20. They not only describe our latest versatile anesthesia machine models, but also present how effectively they operate. From the reports, you may easily see how much our customers enjoy using the models.

If you send us the relevant details, we'll be happy to suggest what specific model you need. We are also enclosing a copy of our current catalog in which page 10 provides you with information about installation and technical training services. With 30 years of manufacturing and marketing in this field, we are sure that the designing and building of such equipment will offer you the most convenience and efficiency in your work.

Should you have any further questions, please let us know. We are always ready to help you.

Sincerely yours,
George Smith

Sample 3 An Unsolicited Sales Letter for Wave Radio and Wave Radio/CD

Bose Corporation

Dept. DMG-T477, The Mountain, Fromingham

MA 01701-8168 USA

May 14, 2015

Dear Sir or Madame,

All men are created equal, but all radios are not!

Most small radios leave a lot to be desired — rich, lifelike sound, for instance. That's why Bose, the most respected name in sound, created the Bose Wave radio and Wave radio/CD. They literally redefine tabletop radio, and they sound as rich and lifelike as many full-sized systems, despite their small sizes.

The key to the Wave radio's high-fidelity sound is our patented acoustic wave-guide speaker technology. Just as a flute strengthens a breath of air to fill an entire concert hall, the wave-guide produces room-filling sound from the Wave radio's small enclosure. The result, according to Radio World, is "a genuine breakthrough in improved sound quality."

The Wave radio/CD is available directly from Bose. So call 1-800-375-2073, ext. T4777, to learn more about our in-home trial and 100% satisfaction guarantee. When you call, be sure to ask about our convenient six-month installment payment plan. If you love music, call today. Because you haven't truly heard radio until you've heard the Bose Wave radio and Wave radio/CD.

Call today, 1-800-375-2073, ext. T4777.

Sincerely,

Raymond Carver

Sales Manager

Sample 4 An Unsolicited Sales Letter for a Training Program

Aresty Institute of Executive Education

The Wharton Business School, University of Pennsylvania

Philadelphia, PA 19104 USA

June 3, 2014

Dear Entrepreneurs,

To successfully drive your business, you must be competitively focused and customer focused. It's a lesson too many people forget.

George Day, marketing professor of the Wharton Business School, University of Pennsylvania has introduced "market-driven strategy" to be the business vocabulary — only one of the many innovative ideas developed by our world-class faculty.

As the oldest business school in the world, Wharton has been at the frontier of finance, international business, management, strategy and marketing. Driven by a faculty with unparalleled depth and breadth, Wharton continues to help organizations negotiate the tricky turns of our increasingly global environment.

This rich tradition of innovation is the foundation of our executive programs, which incorporate a unique blend of scholarly excellence and real-world pragmatism. These insightful, dynamic courses offer the opportunity to refocus and refuel.

Are you running low on new ideas? Come to Wharton Executive Education. You will put what you learn into action and quickly pull away from the field.

Visit us on the web-site http://wh-execed.wharton.upenn.edu/2463.cfm or call us at 1-215-898-1776.

Yours sincerely,
John Carroll
Marketing Director

II. Related Expressions

(1) Planning to buy... ?
   您计划要购买……吗?

(2) Give us a couple of minutes to tell you about...
   占用您几分钟，向您介绍一下……

(3) We feel you will be interested in the new product...
   我们相信您会对我们的新产品……感兴趣。

(4) Please order without delay since our popular products may well be out of stock soon.
   由于我们这些很畅销的货物可能脱销，请从速订购。

(5) A 15% further discount is usually offered for an order for 300 units or more.
   如果订货在 300 台或 300 台以上，我们通常再打 15% 的折扣。

(6) May I make an appointment, Mr. Mahoney, to discuss course content, prices, and times?
   麦哈尼先生，我可否与您会晤以便商讨课程内容、学费及时间问题?

(7) Simply return the enclosed order form and let Spellgram improve the efficiency of your company's English language communication.

您只需寄回随信附带的订单，就可以让拼写软件提高贵公司英语语言交流的效率。

(8) Our company will also enjoy excellent sales prospects in the American market next year.

我们公司明年在美国的市场销售前景会很光明。

(9) Wear our new-style dress, and you will look absolutely smart.

穿上我们的新潮服装，您会显得无比潇洒。

(10) Don't miss the wonderful opportunity to enjoy the finest canned food you'll ever taste.

一定不要错过品尝最美味罐头食品的大好机会！

(11) Don't you want to increase your profits without investing extra fund? If yes, why not bring our products into your business expansion plan?

您想增加营业额而又无须投入额外资金吗？那么，为什么不将我们的产品纳入您的业务扩充计划中呢？

(12) Here's your chance to know THE GLOBE that will bring you news from all over the world every week.

您有机会认识 THE GLOBE 啦！每周它能给您带来世界各地的消息。

(13) Are you having trouble getting your important documents formatted correctly?

您在为您的重要文件编排格式烦恼吗？

(14) According to recent surgeon General's report, by 2020, one half of Americans over 50 may be at risk for fractures from osteoporosis and low bone mass.

根据最近的外科医师总长的报告，到2020年，超过半数以上的美国人可能因骨质疏松和骨量低而有骨折的风险。

(15) Our goods are of superior quality but moderately price. It is 10% lower than that from other suppliers, which facilitate you to push sales in your market.

我方产品质量上乘，价格公道，比其他供应商提供的产品低10%，这更有利于贵公司在你方市场推销。

III. Functional Sentences

(1) You would like to turn your house — cleaning chores into a pleasant activity, wouldn't you? But how? Our Wuchen Vacuum Cleaner can do just that.

你一定想把清扫房间的杂物变成一项令人愉快的活动，是不是？但要怎样才能做到呢？我们的"无尘"真空器可以帮你做到这点。

(2) Just imagine how comfortable it will be when you stretch out your tired limbs on our newly developed White-Cloud water bed?

想象一下吧，当你把疲劳的四肢伸展在我们新研制的白云牌水床垫上该有多么舒适？

(3) Our Figure Master calculator weighs only 1 ounce. It is as heavy as a flashlight. As to its size, the dimensions are 3 1/4 by 2 1/4 by 1/4 inches — only slightly bigger than a playing card. That is why people prefer to bring one wherever they go. It easily fits their purse or jacket pocket.

我们生产的数字王计算器重量仅一盎司，与闪光灯一样重。至于体积大小，它的尺寸为 3 1/4×2 1/4×1/4 英寸——只比一张扑克牌稍微大一点。这就是为什么人们走到哪里都愿意带着它的原因。因为它完全适合装入钱包或夹克口袋中。

(4) If for any reasons you find the model machine unsuitable to your needs, we will replace your order or refund you.

如果因为任何原因您发现这种模型机不适合您的需要，我们将更换您的订货或给您退款。

(5) Order it now, and you'll see a 35% cost cut in your next bill by using your newly purchased heating saver.

如果现在订货，您下次账单上新买的节热器的金额实际会减少 35%。

(6) We thank you for your inquiry about our newly designed office furniture. It is a great pleasure to serve you again.

感谢您对我们新设计的办公设备的询问。很荣幸能够再次为您服务。

(7) This is an unusual opportunity for you to get an unusual product. I am looking forward to receiving your initial order as soon as possible.

这是一次获得非同寻常产品的难得机会。我期待着能尽快接到您的第一份订单。

(8) Our employment service center has over 100 years of experience in placing people like you in jobs. We have contacts with every major corporation and public service in this area.

我们的就业服务中心已有 100 多年为您这样的人寻找工作的经验。我们和本地区每一家大公司及公共服务部门都有联系。

(9) In view of the huge demand of this article, we would advise you to work fast and place an order with us as soon as possible.

鉴于市场对该产品的巨大需求，我方建议贵公司尽快作出决定，尽早下订单。

(10) They are not only as low-priced as the goods of other makers, but they are distinctly superior in the following respects.

同其他供应商提供的商品一样，该商品价格低廉，但在下列方面却更显其独特优势。

(11) Our competitive prices, superior quality and efficiency have won confidence and goodwill among our business clients.

我们具有竞争力的价格、上乘的质量和卓越的效率已经在我们的客户中赢得信誉。

(12) We guarantee to pay all the charges of sending the machine to you and of your returning it, after a thorough trial, if you are not convinced that it will suit you.

我方保证，如果经过通盘试销，你方仍觉得不合适，我方会支付运送机器的来回一切费用。

(13) From the 1st of next month, the price of these goods will be raised from $100 to $150. To get the advantage of the special price, it is necessary to send your order at once.

从下月 1 日起，这些商品的价格都要从 100 美元上调到 150 美元。为了抓住这次特价的机会，请立即寄送订单。

(14) The goods you need are out of stock at present. It is in the consideration of our interests that we'd like to recommend the following substitute form stock and we could arrange shipment in due time.

由于所需的品种目前无货供应，我们想推荐下列库存产品，可以即装，我们这一推荐是照顾双方利益的。

(15) The hand bags we quote are made of superior leathers, with various styles and colors, and can meet the requirements of your market.

我们所报的手提包均用最好的皮革制造，并可供应多种式样及颜色，以适合你们地区的要求。

(16) Act today. Those who order by September 20 will receive 150 oriental-design Christmas cards free.

今天赶紧行动。在 9 月 20 日前订货的顾客将得到 150 张免费的东方风格的圣诞卡。

(17) We can assure you that, for any trial order you may send us, the goods will be carefully selected as if you personally made the choice.

我方保证会为你方寄送来的订单认真挑选产品，如你方亲自选择一样。

(18) Call us toll-free at 800-284-0534 to place your order but if you want more information before your order, the enclosed postage paid card will bring you a complete catalog of our new products.

请拨免费电话 800-284-0534 订货，如您想在订货之前了解更多信息的话，只需把随函谨附的免费明信片寄给我们就可以得到我们最新产品的整套资料。

(19) Let our company help you out. Our experts are pleased to be at your disposal and we own the full-series security equipment suitable for various lines of business.

让我们公司来为您解忧。我们的专家将热诚为您服务，而且我们有适合各行业的全系列的安全设备。

(20) Don't hesitate any more, and hurry up to take action. You should only fill in the blanks below the letter, put into the envelop and then send back to us.

不要迟疑，现在就行动吧。您只需填写信件下方的内容并装入信封随信寄回给我们即可。

Part V Displaying Your Prowess Fully

I. Draft a sales letter according to the hints given below in Chinese.

(1) 产品测试表明，在夏天使用 Glux 牌空调能够使办公室工作人员的工作效率提高 10%；

(2) 工作人员效率的提高意味着利润的增加，从而使成本能迅速收回；

(3) 产品的价格十分有竞争力，比市场上的同类产品低 5%；

(4) 可以分期付款，期限为两年；

(5) 可以电话联系，我们将派技术人员上门安装服务。

II. Rearrange the following numbered paragraphs so that they will read logically in a sales letter.

(1) For dozens of yuan each month can buy peace of mind for your wife and children, and for yourself.

(2) A client of mine is happier today than he has been for a long time. For the first time since he got married 10 years ago, he says that he feels really comfortable about the future. Should he die within the following 30 years, his family will be provided for. His wife would receive 1000 *yuan* per month for a full 30 years, and than lump sum of 100,000 *yuan*.

(3) Such protection would have been beyond his reach a year ago, but now a new insurance plan has enabled him to ensure this security for his family.

(4) Let me know if you like to know the details of the plan. I will call you anytime you like.

III. Draft a sales letter according to the hints given below in English.

(1) Our Bamboo Products are skillfully braided in bright colors and in attractive styles.

(2) Useful and economical.

(3) Push forward to a new stage of technical innovation and new products creation.

(4) Offer a great variety of attractions, Bread Plate, Fruit Box, Flower Basket, Bed,

Table, Chair, Book Stand, Pencil Holder, Vase, Lamp Shade, Bird Cage, etc.

(5) Prices are lower; quality is not inferior to any in the market.

IV. Complete the following sales letter by translating the given Chinese in the brackets into English.

Dear Sirs,

One will certainly feel pleased with ladies' dresses which are ___(1)___ (式样优美、款式优雅、色泽和谐、做工考究). These are just the characteristics of our ladies' dresses for export.

___(2)___ (我公司经营的女装品种繁多). They are long skirts and lounging pajamas suggestive of the tamarisks; gowns and skirts as gorgeous as red roses; embroidered and mandarin dresses, coats and jackets, some in resemblance to the magnificence of peony, others emblematic of the pureness of orchid. Beautiful yet demure, rich but not loud, they are all ___(3)___ (无论在选用衣料、设计剪裁，以及一针一线，均经精心制作).

The inspiration directed toward creative ideas by our manufacturers and the continuous efforts of dealing in this line by our corporation have brought success to all customers of our ladies' dresses.

___(4)___ (此前已寄上出口产品目录一册，谅已收到). Please let us have your specific inquiry enabling us to dispatch samples and make quotations.

Faithfully yours,
Kate Wang

V. Write a sales letter according to the hints given below in Chinese.

商品名称：恩博（ABEL）牌电脑

商品优点：物美价廉，质量非凡

功能全面：无论你在何时何地，甚至旅行时，它都能记录下你的口头指示；非常快捷地改正错误记录；轻松地输出你的打字稿用以邮寄；能为工程技术制作图表和进行设计；当你无聊时它能给你带来乐趣。

售后服务：我们的售后服务确保顾客所需，并能持续操作运行。

随附价目表一份。希望贵公司的首次订货为双方以后的合作带来机会。

Press Release

Part I Warm-up Case Study

Fasten your belt! You can begin an exciting journey towards learning to write a press release efficiently by reading the following sample press release. While studying the sample, you need to discuss its function, components, types and writing style. Finally, you are expected to explore the writing techniques on drafting a press release in a professional way. Now let's come to the following sample.

British Telecom

District Office Telephone House Charter Square Sheffield S1 1BA

Tel 789012   Fax 789123

March 1, 2006

Publication Date: March 6, 2006

COMPUTERIZED TELEPHONE EXCHANGE AT LINCOLN

From today, all British Telecom customers in the city of Lincoln can reap the benefit offered by their new, fully computerized telephone exchange.

At 7:00 a.m., the final stage in a two-year £1.5 million project was reached, when the remaining 10,000 lines were transferred onto the new digital exchange.

Now, all 25,000 customers can look forward to faster connections, clearer calls, with

> fewer wrong numbers or crossed lines, and take advantage of a host of exciting new facilities known as Star Services.
>
> In addition, optional itemized bills at no extra cost will ensure that customers can keep a track of their calls.
>
> District Exchange Services Manager, John Lashmar, commented "I am delighted to see this extensive modernization program come to fruition in Lincoln. It will enable BT to offer first-class communications service to all its customers in the city."
>
> -End-
>
> Contact: Ron Gee, Press Relations Manager; Sheffield Tel (0742)708267

Have you got some ideas about how to write a press release after studying the above sample? If so, you are expected to do a brief analysis of the above sample and write down the key points.

KEY POINTS HERE

_____
_____
_____
_____
_____
_____
_____
_____

Part II Having a Clear Picture

I. Concept of Press Release

A press release is a written or recorded communication directed at members of the news media for the purpose of announcing something claimed as having news value. Relocation of offices, introduction of new products, exciting technological breakthrough, purchase of new equipment or building, changes of top personnel etc. are commonly announced in press releases. Typically, it is mailed or faxed to assignment editors at newspapers, magazines, radio stations, television stations and television networks. And now it is common to see companies releasing their news on the Internet.

II. Components of Press Releases

1. Letterhead

The press release is usually typed on sheets of paper with letterhead, which typically comprises the name, address and the telephone number of the news source.

2. Release Instructions

This section includes in a few words directives as to when the information can be released. There are several different forms of release date. "FOR IMMEDIATE RELEASE" is the usual form to be used in writing. Be sure to make those words appear in the upper left-hand margin, just under your letterhead. And you should also capitalize every letter. In addition, some may use "FOR RELEASE month, day, year" or "FOR RELEASE AT WILL". No matter which form you use, you should send your press release out well in advance.

3. Media Contact Information

Right under the release instruction, you should list the contact information left-justified. Contact information should include the name, title, telephone and fax numbers of your company contact person, company name, e-mail address, and the website address. It is important to give the home number of the contact person since reporters often work on deadlines and may not be available until after hours.

4. Headline

Skip two lines after your contact information and briefly summarize the news. This headline is one of the most important components of the press release as it needs to grab the attention of the editor. It should be written in bold type and a font that is larger than the body text. Preferred type fonts are Arial, Times New Roman, or Verdana. Keep the headline to 80–125 characters maximum. Usually the headline includes the name of the company issuing the release. However, don't include terms such as "Company" "Incorporated" "Limited" or their abbreviations unless they are necessary to distinguish the organization from another of a similar name. Don't use exclamation points or dollar signs.

5. Dateline

The dateline should include the city and state where the press release issued from and the date it is being released. You should always start the dateline in the following format: City, State (or Country) — Date. Ensure that the date you use is current when submitting.

Media outlets won't want what would appear to be old news.

6. Introduction

The first paragraph of the release should be written in a clear and concise manner. The opening sentence contains the most important information; keep it to 25 words or less. Never take it for granted that the reader has read your headline. It should contain relevant information to your message such as the five W's (who, what, when, where, why). Remember, your story must be newsworthy and factual; don't make it a sales pitch or it will end up in the trash.

7. Body

The main body of your press release should include pertinent information about your product, service or event. If writing about a product, make sure to include details on when the product is available, where it can be purchased and what the cost is. If writing about an event, include the date, location of the event and any other pertinent information. In addition, do remember that you should keep your sentences and paragraphs short; a paragraph should have no more than 3 or 4 sentences. Your release should be 500 to 800 words, written in a word processing program, and spell-checked for errors.

Usually, in the last paragraph of the body, some will put additional information such as contact × × × (contact person in your company) or visit www. × × × × (your URL).com.

8. Ending

At the end of the press release, you need to indicate that the release is ended. This lets the journalists know they have received the entire release. Type "End" or "# # #" on the first line after your text is completed. If your release goes over one page, type "MORE" or "CONTINUED" at the bottom of the first page and use a one-word "slug" to indicate that it is the second page of the release. For example, a press release about logging issues in the Pacific Northwest might use the slug "logging/page 2".

III. Language Features of Press Releases

(1) Speak plainly with ordinary language;

(2) Use active verbs to enliven your release;

(3) Do not exaggerate your news or use too many adjectives. Try to use more basic, clear words instead;

(4) Avoid first person perspective and the passive voice;

(5) Avoid marketing tone. Do not advertise your product. Instead, stick to the facts;

(6) Make sure that you have written permission before including information or quotes from employees or affiliates of other companies.

Part III Showing Your Talent Slightly

Now that you have had a clear picture of the components and language features of press releases, you can fulfill the following situational task with the help of the Warm-up Case Study.

I. Situational Task

You work as an office clerk in Public Relations Department, ABC Corporation. This morning, Mr. Li Gang, the Department Chief asks you to draft a copy of press release announcing the following information about ABC Corporation.

(1) In March, 20___, it was listed as the world's largest contractor by the American "Engineering Journalists".

(2) In 20___, it signed $334 million contracts and produced $438 million business turnover.

(3) Performance in exploring overseas markets in 2014.

a. Opened an overseas business department to coordinate among its organizations overseas;

b. Hong Kong branch: fulfilled a $184 million contractual volume and a $110 million business turnover;

c. Macao branch: fulfilled a $1.44 million contractual volume, 14 times more than the previous year's plan.

II. Do It Yourself

Issued by ABC Corporation

ABC Corporation World's 76th Largest Contractor

_____
_____
_____
_____
_____
_____
_____
_____
_____

Part IV Opening the Treasure Box

I. Samples

Sample 1

> FOR IMMEDIATE RELEASE
> Contact Name: John McGah
> Contact Phone: 617-287-5532
>
> **Party for a Purpose at Paddy Burke's Pub**
> **Part of the Banding Together to End Homelessness Series:**
> Benefit for Boston-based national homelessness public awareness project
>
> The documentary and educational program *Give Us Your Poor: Homelessness & the United States* is partnering with the Boston's Paddy Burke's Pub and local businesses for a March 20th benefit evening of fun, food, drinks, and entertainment to help fight homelessness nationally and locally.
>
> ***BANDING TOGETHER TO END HOMELESSNESS*** at Paddy Burke's Pub in Boston near the Fleet Center, from 7:00–12:00 p.m., will feature the original rock and roll music of Linus and an opening acoustic set by the singers of New York's Spacecake. Comedian Joe LaRoche will be emceeing the evening. Tickets are $20 or $15 with a college ID (donations greatly appreciated). Raffles and inexpensive drinks will be part of the evening. Raffles include "Beer for a Year" donated by Sam Adams and "Ice Cream for a Year" donated by Brigham's Ice Cream.
>
> *The Give Us Your Poor* is revolutionizing awareness of the structural causes of homelessness to stimulate real, effective solutions. *Give Us Your Poor* is developing a documentary, educational materials, and community organizations to change how America views its homeless. The project is based at UMass Boston's Center for Social Policy.
>
> *Give Us Your Poor* has already garnered contributions and support from world-class musicians, filmmakers, and homeless advocacy organizations — including music by Bruce Springsteen, Sting, Arlo Guthrie, John Mellencamp — Academy Award®-winning filmmakers One Arts, leading scholars, homeless people, former New York City Mayor David Dinkins, Ellen Bassuk, and the National Coalition for the Homeless.
>
> For more information visit the event webpage on *Give Us Your Poor's* website: www. GiveUsYourPoor. Org/PaddyBurkes

Sample 2

THE L&L GROUP TO PURCHASE SOUTHERN ATHLETIC

Dateline: May 27, 2007　　Troy, MI
Contact Name: John Levy, Chairman, L&L Enterprises
Contact Phone: (248)689-3850
Contact Fax: (248)689-4652

TROY, MI—May 27, 2003—The L&L Group of Troy, Michigan, owners of the REACH Athletic and Union Jacks labels, announced on Tuesday it has signed a definitive agreement with Russsell Corporation providing for the purchase of the SOUTHERN ATHLETIC trademark and related assets. The Southern Athletic brand has been licensed to L&L since May 2006 and now L&L has completed the sale of the brand.

Southern Athletic will manufacture a complete line of baseball/softball uniforms for 2008 in addition to its current basketball and volleyball uniform categories. "Southern Athletic will be a superb addition to our product lines", said John Levy, chairman and CEO. "We will offer our customers a consistent, competitive, quality line of team uniforms, specializing in on-time delivery to our recreational and team dealers."

About L&L Group

The L&L Group, privately held and formed in 1948, owns Auto City Candy, Foremost Athletic, L&L Concession Co., Reach Athletic and Union Jacks Soccer.

About Southern Athletic

Southern Athletic was the original uniform maker in Knoxville, TN prior to Colgate Palmolive changing it to Bike Athletic in 1976.

For more information, contact:
John Levy, Chairman, L&L Enterprises
1307 E. Maple Road
Troy, MI 48083

Phone: (248)689-3850

Fax: (248)689-4652

###

Sample 3

FOR IMMEDIATE RELEASE

Contact information:

Martin Johnson

1-388-693-5772

E-mail: martin@left-teegolf.com

Website: http://www.left-teegolf.com

Left-Tee Golf.com Announces Version 3.5 of Its Internet Portal for Lefty Golfers

EVERETT, Wash.—July 2, 2006—Left-Tee Golf.com LLC, an Internet portal for left-handed golfers, has launched a new version of their website which features the Internet's only combined auctions and classified area for left-handed golf equipment sales and trades.

"Left-Tee Golf. com already has a strong presence in the online golf community for lefty golfers", said Left-Tee Golf.com President and Founder Martin Johnson. "The user interface and navigation of version 3.5 enables us to enrich our users' online experience."

Additional features on the site include editorial content and golf tips from left-handed PGA professionals, exclusive live chats, and a marketplace for buyers and sellers of new and used equipment. The site will also feature a diary following the progress of left-handed LPGA Tour player Angela Buzminski.

"The enhancement of the content and services area of our website, along with the new marketplace feature, widens the gap between ourselves and other lefty golfers related websites", Johnson adds.

About Left-Tee Golf.com

> Founded in April 2000, Left-Tee Golf.com is the Internet's most comprehensive resource for left-handed golfers. With over 1000 registered members worldwide and a network of over 150 left-handed PGA Teaching Professionals, the company has developed the Internets only online community for left-handed golfers. For more information, visit http://www. Left-teegolf.com.
>
> ###

II. Related Expressions

(1) ... today announced that...　……今天宣布……

(2) ... has received the approval of...　……获得了……的批准

(3) ... is expected to be operational in the fourth quarter of...
　　……预期将于……第四季度开始运作。

(4) Under the terms of the agreement,...　协议规定……

(5) By uniting the complementary strengths of these two organizations, we will...
　　通过两个机构的优势互补，我们将……

(6) ... are available for purchase at...　可以从……购买……

(7) For more information on... , please contact...
　　如想获得关于……更多的信息，请联系……

(8) For more information on... or to purchase, please visit...
　　如想获得关于……更多的信息或购买我们的产品，请登录……

(9) ... has owned a wide range of product groups of... categories with over... specifications including...
　　……已拥有……大门类……个规格品种的产品群，包括……

(10) ... is a young, burgeoning, open and internationalized company.
　　……是一家年轻的、新兴的、开放的国家化公司。

(11) ... growth rate ranked 1st, exceeding the world famous cosmetics firms of Germany and Japan.
　　……的增长速度名列榜首，超过了德国、日本等世界著名的化妆品企业。

(12) Since our incorporation in 2000, this company is committed to ethical marketing practices and professional service.
　　自 2000 年建立以来，我们一直采用合乎道德的营销方式，并提供专业的服务。

(13) If you need more information, please contact our Customer Service Department at 123-83920047.

如果您需要更多的信息，请联系我公司客户服务部，电话：123-83920047。

(14) As a professional textile dealer, this company promises that it will always strive to offer the best products and services to our clients.

作为专业的纺织品经销商，本公司向您承诺，我们会一直努力为客户提供最好的产品和服务。

(15) This company would like to build a close cooperation relationship with you, in exploring the tremendous opportunities in the tourism industry.

我们希望与您建立紧密的合作关系，一起探索旅游业所蕴含的巨大商机。

III. Functional Sentences

(1) We will create a new entity with economic potential far greater than what we could achieve individually.

我们将开创一个比我们独立运作更具经济潜力的联合体。

(2) The company will be based in Antwerp, and will market coolant products to original equipment manufacturers, petroleum companies, independent mass marketers.

该公司将以安特卫普为基地，向原设备生产商、原油公司、独立经销商提供制冷剂。

(3) To celebrate our successful growth over the past year, we wanted to give back to our clients and make them feel renewed going into the summer.

为了庆祝在过去一年所取得的成就，我们想以此回馈我们的消费者，让他们以新的面貌迎接夏天的到来。

(4) The salon opened in 1998 and has become known for its creative team of dedicated stylists and skin care experts.

这家沙龙始创于1998年并以其富有创新和献身精神的设计师和皮肤护理专家团队而闻名。

(5) The loyalty to the users and the popularity enjoyed by the products are closely linked.

用户的忠诚度与产品的美誉度是紧密联系的。

(6) This Company's pioneering work over the past 16 years has formed a developing framework of an international enterprise which is a competitive global design net, manufacturing net, and a sales service net.

本公司16年的创业之路搭建起一个国际化企业的发展框架，即一个有竞争力的全球设计网络、制造网络、营销与服务网络。

(7) With its rapid development, Haier's products are enjoying higher and higher popularity and prestige in the world market.

在规模迅速发展的同时，海尔在国际市场的品牌美誉度和影响力也在迅速提高。

(8) Rooted in the increasingly competitive electronics market, this Company takes creativity as its core spirit, sparing no efforts to meet the needs of the users and their potential demand.

在日益竞争的电子市场，本公司以创新为核心，最大程度地满足用户需求及潜在需求。

(9) We have a long history, rich experience and reliable reputation.

本公司历史悠久，经验丰富，信誉可靠。

(10) We sincerely wish to strengthen business relations with counterparts both at home and abroad.

我们真诚地希望与国内外同行加强业务联系。

(11) The company is recognized as one of the pioneers of engineering industry and has achieved EU Safety Certification, ISO9001 International Quality Standard and ISO14001 for its Environment Management System Certification.

本公司被誉为机械行业先驱之一，并通过了欧盟安全认证、ISO9001 国际质量标准认证和 ISO14001 环境管理体系认证。

(12) At present, we have four production bases; one based in Shanghai and others in Shenzhen, Xiamen and Tianjin. In addition, we have representative agencies and service centers in 50 countries.

当前，我们拥有 4 个生产基地，一个在上海，其他分别位于深圳、厦门和天津。此外，我们还在全球 50 个国家设有办事处和服务中心。

(13) This company is well-known for its famous brand, quality products, competitive price, effective service and energy-saving machinery, all of which have led to our business expanding around the globe.

本公司以名优品牌、优质产品、有竞争力的价格、高效的服务以及节能机械设备而闻名，所有这些优势使我们的业务遍及全球。

(14) With the rapid development of 20 years, this company has become one of the largest engineering machinery manufacturers over the world, enjoying an annual operation revenue of 20 billion dollars.

经过 20 年的快速发展，本公司已经成为世界上最大的工程机械制造商之一，年营业收入达到 200 亿美元。

(15) Since its foundation in 2001, this company has established a mature system of services in tourism.

自 2001 年成立以来，本公司已经建立了一个成熟的旅游服务体系。

(16) Through its unique business model, this company is able to integrate the primary business requirements to serve the consumers effectively.

通过其独特的经营模式，本公司能够将主要的商业需求一体化，从而为顾客提供高效的服务。

(17) This company is committed to delivering high quality products and services to all our industrial clients, and thus we become a totally reliable partner with your business.

本公司长期致力于为我们的工业客户提供优质的产品和服务，并就此成为可信任的合作伙伴。

(18) With our accumulation of experience and abundant resources all over the world, we are able to offer our clients the newest products with the highest quality and competitive prices.

由于拥有丰富的经验和遍布全世界的丰富资源，我们能够为我们的客户提供质量最好、价格最合理的新产品。

(19) Located in Tianjin, this company is Sino-American joint venture, which provides technological solutions to the problems of air pollution.

本公司是一家位于天津的中美合资企业，主营业务是就空气污染问题提供技术解决方案。

(20) This company specializes in researching and developing applications for disinfecting waste water using environmentally safe, cost-effective alternatives to ozonization.

本公司主要研究和开发废水消毒的专业设计方案——应用环保、成本低、效益高的替代品取代臭氧化法。

Part V Displaying Your Prowess Fully

I. Rearrange the following paragraphs into a press release about NASA awards contract.

SUPER SEC TRAINING CENTER

21 Exeter Road #07-04 Grange Tower Singapore 1922

Tel: 6229837 Fax: 6229324 E-mail: sstc@sing net.com.sg

PRESS RELEASE

September 2, 2008

PUBLICATION DATE: September 12, 2008

OPEN DAY SHOWS SUPER SEC MOVES WITH THE TIMES

(1) Demonstrations will be given on the school's recently-installed computers as well as the fax machine.

(2) Tours of the school will be arranged for visitors to see the new, well-stocked library as well as innovative wall displays showing examples of the work of the college.

(3) Super Sec Training Center are certainly incorporating new technology into their courses, and visitors are encouraged to see their additional and improved facilities at their Open House on Wednesday September 14.

(4) Refreshments will be provided throughout the day to all visitors at Super Sec's Open House, which will be held from 10:00 a.m. to 8:00 p.m. on Wednesday September 14.

(5) Visitors will also be able to look at projects and exhibits which Super Sec students have been working on over the last few months.

-End-

Contact: Miss Jenny King, Registrar. Tel: 6229345

II. You work as a PR Manager at a French company, Trans-European Haulage Ltd. You have received such a phone call: "This is International Business News. We hear from you the Haulage Drivers' Union that they intend raising with the Minister the business of the sacking of your British drivers in France because you say a Ministry of Labor official there told you to employ Frenchmen instead. Is this true?" Therefore, you need to draft a press release on *the Thames* to clarify the incident of your company's recent dismissal of four British drivers. The letter-head, date and contact person are given as follows:

TRANS-EUROPEAN HAULAGE LTD
18-22 Castle Street, Dover, England
Tel: 234-4533

PRESS RELEASE

March 1, 2006

BRITISH DRIVERS SACKED

_____
_____
_____
_____
_____
_____

-End-

Contact: Miss Burns, Trans-European Haulage Ltd. Tel: 234-9374

III. Fill in the blanks of the following press release with the appropriate forms of the words and expressions given in the box.

> challenge; beauty products; locate; in a row; honor; cater to;
> for more information; gross revenue; submit a description; commit to;
> style and service; exceed expectation; fee renewed; change your look

FOR IMMEDIATE RELEASE

Contact Information: Emily Brown Right On Communications

Voice: 760-591-0700

E-mail: emilybn@rightonc.com

Website: http://www.rightonc.com

NORTH COUNTY SALON CELEBRATES NATIONAL AWARD WITH MAKEOVER MADNESS CONTEST

ESCONDIDO, CA — February 14, 2007 — The Loft Hair Design & Skin Care, ____(1)____ at 106 West Grand Avenue in Escondido, has been named a Top 200-fastest growing salon for the second year ____(2)____ by *Salon Today* magazine. In appreciation to its clients and North County residents, the salon has ____(3)____ with a Makeover Madness contest. Chosen participants will receive a new cut and color, relaxing facial, eyebrow and make-up application plus $75 worth of ____(4)____.

"Spring time is the perfect season to ____(5)____. To celebrate our successful growth over the past year, we wanted to give back to our clients and make them ____(6)____ going into the summer," says Michelle Cruise, the owner of The Loft Hair Design & Skin Care.

To participate, customers must ____(7)____ and a photo of why they or a friend deserves a makeover. Send to http://www.theloft hairdesign.com/joininthefunform.html. All participants will be chosen by March 31, 2007.

The Salon Today 200 Award ____(8)____ salon with the highest increase in year over year gross sales and who maintained this growth through 2006. In South California, only six salons received this award. During 2006, The Loft Hair Design & Skin Care increased ____(9)____ by 32%.

About the Loft

A 2006 national Top 200 salon, the Loft Hair Design & Skin Care is North County's premier salon for ___(10)___. The salon opened in 1998 and has become known for its creative team of dedicated stylists and skin care experts.

The owner, Shawna Cruise, has worked in the beauty industry for 17 years and oversees a team of qualified individuals that ___(11)___ a hip and savvy clientele. Her mission is to create a client experience that consistently ___(12)___. The Loft Hair Design is ___(13)___ the integrity of each service through professional education, creativity, communication, and a deep appreciation for each client.

The Loft Hair Design is located in downtown Escondido at 106 West Grand Avenue. ___(14)___, call 726-785-LOFT.

###

IV. Rearrange the following paragraphs into a press release, and then form a complete press release by using the format introduced in this unit.

Release Instruction: Friday, August 28, 2008

Source of News: the Elf Group & Texaco

Headline: Texaco and Elf Lubrifiants Announce Formation of European Coolants Joint Venture

Main Body:

(1) The company will be based in Antwerp, and will market coolant products to original equipment manufacturers, petroleum companies, independent blenders and mass marketers. However, the respective sales organizations of Elf and Texaco will continue to supply under their own brand through the retail distribution channel. The companies do not expect any impact on employment levels as a result of the formation of this joint venture.

(2) In a joint statement concerning the venture, President & GM of Texaco Global Products LLC, Thomas S. Neslge, and Elf Lubrifiants President Jean-Jaques Mosconi, said, "By uniting the complementary strengths of these two organizations, we will become the second largest marketer of antifreeze/coolants and also number two supplier to the original equipment manufacturers throughout Europe. We will create a new entity with economic potential far greater than what we could achieve individuality. The result will be a company with the ability to provide our customers with the highest quality products coupled with a long term commitment to superior levels of service and technical support."

(3) No other assets or businesses of either Texaco or Elf are included in this new company.

(4) The new entity combines the significant technical, manufacturing and marketing

strengths of Texco and Elf, resulting in operating efficiencies that will serve as a platform for growth throughout this important market. The joint venture has received the approval of the Commission of the European Communities and is expected be operational in the fourth quarter of 2008.

(5) Under the terms of the agreement, Texaco's worldwide research laboratory in Ghent, Belgium will provide the technical support and perform the fundamental research for the venture. Coolant production will be provided from the venture's modern and flexible blending plant located at Elf's manufacturing facility in Antwerp, Belgium.

(6) Houston and Paris, Aug. 8, 2008 — Texaco and Elf lubrifiants today announced that their subsidiary companies, S.A. Texaco Belgium N.V. and Elf Oil Belgium N.V., have agreed to form a 50/50 joint venture company that will manufacture and market automotive, commercial and industrial coolants throughout Europe.

V. Translate the following press release into Chinese.

Huawei, Website Undergoes Successful IPv6 Test Run as Part of World IPv6 Day

[Shenzhen, China, June 8, 2011]

Huawei, a leading telecom solutions provider, announced that it enabled IPv6 on its main website (www.huawei.com) during the Internet Society's (ISOC) World IPv6 Day on June 8, and that the test run was a success.

World IPv6 Day was organized by ISOC and major content providers to test public IPv6 deployment during a coordinated 24-hour test period. Huawei and over 400 other participants took part, working together to promote, publicize, and apply IPv6 technology in order to ensure an eventual smooth, wide-scale evolution from IPv4 to IPv6.

On World IPv6 Day, the official websites of all participants provided access services for IPv6 users as well as IPv4 users. The event aimed to monitor the stability, reliability, and security of IPv6 networks and services by increasing the number of IPv6 visitors. The day also served to locate and solve problems before the eventual large-scale application of IPv6 standards, and also to promote the smooth evolution of Internet technology from IPv4 to IPv6.

As one of the leading suppliers of IPv6 network equipment and solutions, in the past, Huawei has cooperated with three of the largest carriers in China and has successfully deployed IPv6 network in several cities including Wuxi, Shenzhen, and Shanghai. In 2005, Huawei provided more than 70 percent of the IPv6 network equipment for China's Next

Generation Internet (CNGI) project, in what at the time amounted to the world's largest IPv6 network, the CNGI project has since been operating smoothly. Furthermore, Huawei's IPv6 network equipment and solutions have been successfully deployed at both the Shanghai World Expo and the China-ASEAN Expo, and will provide network services for the upcoming 2011 Summer Universiade in Shenzhen.

External Corporate Communication

Unit 15

Letter of Congratulation

Part I Warm-up Case Study

Fasten your belt! You can begin an exciting journey towards learning to write a letter of congratulation efficiently by reading the following sample letter. While studying the letter, you need to discuss its function, components, types and writing style. Finally, you are expected to explore the writing techniques on drafting a letter of congratulation in a professional way. Now let's come to the following sample.

> Dear Mr. Wolf,
>
> I have learned with great delight that you have been promoted to sales manager of your company. Congratulations!
>
> With all the hard work you have done and your many years of conscientious efforts, this is all you deserve. Simon & Ford is certainly lucky to have you in charge of its marketing operations.
>
> I wish you every success in managing the affairs of your sales division. My colleagues join me in sending you our hearty congratulations.
>
> Yours faithfully,

Have you got some ideas about how to write a letter of congratulation after studying the above sample? If so, you are expected to do a brief analysis of the above sample and write down the key points.

KEY POINTS HERE

_____
_____
_____
_____
_____
_____
_____

Part II Having a Clear Picture

I. Concept of Letter of Congratulation

Letters of congratulation are used in both personal and business situations, indicating the writer's profound interest in the success or good luck of the recipient. Whatever the occasion is, the letters are certainly to be well received as everyone likes to have accomplishments acknowledged. You need to express congratulations to relatives, friends, colleagues, clients and other business associates about their good news. Congratulation letters add a glow to both personal and business relationship.

II. Components of Letters of Congratulation

Generally speaking, you should always keep in mind the following three parts while writing letters of congratulation: opening, body, and closing.

1. Opening

In this part, you begin with the expression of congratulations, thus clearly stating your purpose of writing the letter. Then you need to state the specific occasion you are referencing and indicate how you heard of the good news, if necessary.

2. Body

It is necessary to mention the reason why you convey your congratulations. In this part you need to further express your praise, approval and discuss the significance of the achievement. In addition, you should tell the recipient how happy, proud or impressed you are.

3. Closing

The expression of goodwill and wishes are included to end your letters of congratulation. For example, you may wish the person continued success or happiness;

express your confidence in further cooperation; assure the recipient of your affection, admiration or continued business support. Sometimes you may also end the letter by reiterating your congratulatory message in the conclusion, such as "Once again, I extend to you my congratulations."

III. Types of Letters of Congratulation

There are many occasions that call for letters of congratulation, for example:

(1) Congratulations on promotion;
(2) Congratulations on anniversary;
(3) Congratulations on new venture;
(4) Congratulations on winning an honor/award;
(5) Congratulations on marriage;
(6) Congratulations on the birth of child;
(7) Congratulations on birthday.

IV. Tips for Letters of Congratulation Writing

(1) The language should always be positive when letters of congratulation are drafted.
(2) Make your letters of congratulation formal and brief.
(3) Personal remarks or references should be contained in the letters of congratulation.

Part III Showing Your Talent Slightly

Now that you have had a clear picture of the components and types of letters of congratulation, you can fulfill the following situational task with the help of the Warm-up Case Study.

I. Situational Task

You work as the sales manager in ABC Co., Ltd. And you heard that Mr. Rockefeller, one of your business associates has been recently promoted to the position of associate general manager of Leading Corporation. Please write a letter of congratulation to him.

II. Do It Yourself

Dear Mr. Rockefeller,

_____
_____
_____
_____

_____
_____
_____
_____

Yours faithfully,

Part IV Opening the Treasure Box

I. Samples

Sample 1 Congratulations on Promotion (1)

> Dear Mr. Henry,
>
> It was with great pleasure that I read of your promotion to the position of manager of the First Company.
>
> It must be a great satisfaction to have achieved a goal toward which you have been working for many years. I am sure your firm has made a very wise choice and that you will excel in your new role.
>
> Please accept my congratulations on your promotion and my very best wishes for your continued success.
>
> Sincerely yours,

Sample 2 Congratulations on Promotion (2)

> Dear Mr. Smith,
>
> I am writing to convey my warm congratulations on your appointment to the Board of Northern Industries Ltd.
>
> My colleagues and I are delighted that years of service you have given to your company should at last have been rewarded in this way. Looking back on your activities so far, we know that your experience and enthusiasm are the essential qualities that are needed for the position. We join in sending you our very best wishes for the future.
>
> Warm regards and best wishes,
>
> Sincerely yours,

Sample 3 Congratulations on Employee's Anniversary

Dear Mary,

July 4th will mark your fifth anniversary as a member of our Shell Company. We would like to take this opportunity to thank you for these past five years of fine workmanship and company loyalty.

We know that the growth and success of our company is largely dependent on having strong and capable staff members like you, and recognize the contribution you make in helping us maintain the position we enjoy in the industry.

We look forward to working with you in the years ahead and would like to offer our congratulations on this anniversary.

Sincerely yours,

Sample 4 Congratulations on a New Venture

Dear Mr. Harmon,

I have learned with great joy that you are opening your consulting firm.

I would like to add my congratulations to the many you must be receiving. With your talent, I'm sure the new firm will be a great success. I sincerely hope you will find in this new venture the happiness and satisfaction you so richly deserve.

With all best wishes,

Yours faithfully,

Sample 5 Congratulations on Winning an Honor (1)

Dear Mr. Chen,

I would like to congratulate you on your being honored by the New Year Honors Committee as one of the outstanding enterprisers. May I add my voice to the chorus of congratulations that you must be hearing from all sides?

Your service to local industry and commerce these years have been quite outstanding. It is indeed gratifying to learn that these have been appropriately rewarded.

Once again, I extend to you my congratulations.

Yours sincerely,

Sample 6 Congratulations on Winning an Honor (2)

Dear Dr. Good,

  I'm very glad to congratulate you on your having received a doctorate in administration. I know this has meant years of study and your hard work rewarded. It's an achievement you can well be proud of. From the excellent academic records you have made, I'm sure that you will be more successful in your career.

  My best wishes to you!

Sincerely yours,

Sample 7 Congratulations on Marriage

Dear Amy and John,

  Congratulations on your recent marriage.

  I wish you both nothing but the very best. You are a perfect match and I was so honored to be a part of your day.

  I send you my love and wish you ever-increasing happiness as the years go by.

  Congratulations again on your September 10, 2018 wedding.

Affectionately,

Sample 8 Congratulations on Birth of Child (1)

Dear Charles,

  The wonderful news about the birth of your son reached me yesterday. Congratulations on your new baby.

  I imagine you just can't wait for all the chaos that having a little baby boy around the house will bring! Please accept my best wishes and hopes that your son will grow up healthy, wealthy and wise.

  I wish you and your family every happiness.

Sincerely yours,

Sample 9 Congratulations on Birth of Child (2)

Dear Paul,

  Congratulations on the birth of your new baby! There is nothing more wonderful or exciting as the entry into the world of a new and promising life. We are all so pleased for you and your family.

    We hope you enjoy these precious moments of babyhood, and that you will give your son a big hug from all of us!

Sincerely yours,

Sample 10 Congratulations on Birthday

Dear Mr. Peon,

    Congratulations on your birthday! I hope that all your years to come will be as happy as those past.

    I'm sending you a little gift as a token of appreciation for your kindness to me, which I hope you will enjoy.

    With kindest regards to you.

Sincerely yours,

II. Related Expressions

(1) excel　　*v.* 优于，擅长，胜过

    excel in your new role　　胜任您的新角色

(2) chorus　　*n.* 齐声，异口同声

(3) extend　　*v.* 给予，提供，延伸

(4) promotion (to)　　*n.* 提升，晋升（为……）

(5) Many years of service you have given to your company should at last have been rewarded in this way.　　您为贵公司服务多年，最终应该获得这样的回报。

(6) essential qualities　　必备的素质条件

(7) company loyalty　　对公司的忠诚度

(8) It is indeed gratifying to learn that these have been appropriately rewarded.

    今悉您获此殊荣，实至名归。

(9) perfect match　　绝配，完美组合

(10) as a token of...　　为了表示……

(11) excellent academic records　　优异的学业成绩

(12) look back on　　回顾

(13) achieve a goal　　达到目标

(14) make a very wise choice　　作出明智选择

III. Functional Sentences

(1) Please accept my sincerest congratulations on your promotion.
请接受我对您升职最真诚的祝贺。

(2) Please accept my congratulations on your being promoted to the position of Sales Manager.
欣悉你荣升为销售经理，请接受我的祝贺。

(3) I would like to express my hearty congratulations to you on your promotion.
对于您的升职，我愿表达我最衷心的祝贺。

(4) Please add my warmest congratulations to the large chorus of friends acclaiming your promotion.
我愿和朋友们一起为你的晋升欢呼。

(5) I would like to extend my congratulations on your great success.
我谨祝贺您获得了巨大成功。

(6) Please accept our warmest congratulations on your appointment.
请接受我们最热烈的祝贺，祝你荣任新职。

(7) Please accept my heartiest congratulations on the happiest event of your life.
请接受我对你一生中最大的喜事表示由衷的祝贺。

(8) Congratulations on your marriage.
祝贺你结婚大喜。

(9) I was really happy to hear that you are opening a new branch.
欣悉贵公司新成立了一家分公司。

(10) The wonderful news about the birth of your daughter has just reached us.
我们刚刚得知你女儿出生的好消息。

(11) Congratulations on your new baby.
祝贺你喜得麟儿。

(12) I hope both mother and daughter are doing well.
我希望母女平安健康。

(13) I can imagine you just can't wait for the chaos that having a little baby around the house will bring.
我能想象出来，你一定渴望感受家里多了一个小生命所带来的忙乱热闹的气氛。

(14) With all the hard work you have done for years, this is all you deserve.
数年来你工作勤勉，这完全是你应得的回报。

(15) The honor will give pleasure to a wide circle of people who know you and your work.

你获此荣誉，所有与你相识或共事的人都感到十分光荣。

(16) My best wishes for your good health and continued success.

祝你身体健康，事业成功。

(17) I'm sure that the future will hold much more for you.

我相信今后你定会大有作为。

(18) With my heartiest congratulations on your promotion and best wishes for your future success.

对你的晋升致以衷心的祝贺，并预祝你取得更大的成就。

(19) I'm sending you hearty greetings on your happy birthday, and many happy returns of the day.

恭贺诞辰，祝您岁岁有今朝。

(20) I hope this little present will add a bit to your happiness on your birthday.

希望这份小礼物能为你的生日增添一点快乐。

(21) Wishing you the best of all good things on your birthday and for the many more to come.

在你生日之际，祝福你拥有最美好的一切，更多美好的未来。

(22) We would like to extend our congratulations and offer our very best wishes for your every success in the business dealings.

特此祝贺，并祝你生意兴隆、事事顺达。

(23) Your enlightened leadership will surely bring in the continuing growth of your company.

您开明而又非凡的领导力一定能带来企业的不断发展与壮大。

(24) It was delightful news for me to learn that you had captured the No. 1 position in sales in the market.

欣悉您的销售额在市场销售份额中名列第一。

Part V Displaying Your Prowess Fully

I. Draft a letter expressing your congratulations on promotion according to the hints given below in Chinese.

你的朋友 Karl 的工作得到了大家的一致认可，并获得了提升的机会，被任命为公司的营销部经理。这则消息刊登在当地一家早报上。请写信对他表示祝贺。

II. Fill in the blanks to complete the letter of congratulation by translating the given Chinese in the brackets into English.

Dear Mr. Harmon,

　　I am very pleased to learn that ___(1)___ （您最近晋升为福特公司的经理。） It must be a great satisfaction to ___(2)___ （实现了您多年努力奋斗的目标）.

Under your leadership Ford Company will, I am sure, ___(3)___ （一定能继续其在商界的良好声誉）.

___(4)___ （对您的晋升致以衷心的祝贺）and best wishes for your continued success.

Yours sincerely,

III. Draft a letter of congratulation according to the hints given below in Chinese.

你的生意伙伴 Mr. Dawson 的广告公司被广告联盟授予全国十佳的荣誉称号。请写信对他表示祝贺。

IV. Translate the following letter into English.

亲爱的亨利：

我们刚刚听到你儿子诞生的好消息。祝贺你！请接受我们最美好的祝福，祝愿他长得像爸爸，聪明、健康、富裕。

谨祝你及家人生活幸福！

真诚的

V. Rearrange the following expressions so that they can compose a letter of congratulation.

(1) so that we can give you our congratulations in person.

(2) Sincerely yours,

(3) Lee and I send you both our love,

(4) We hope you will let us know the time you return home,

(5) and best wishes for every happiness that life may bring you.

(6) Dear Tina and Jerry,

(7) We were so delighted to receive the announcement of your marriage.

VI. Draft a letter of congratulation according to the hints given below in Chinese.

你从当天的早报中得知 Mr. Fang 成立了自己的咨询公司。请写信祝贺他最近新公司开张之喜。

VII. Draft a letter of congratulation according to the hints given below in Chinese.

明天是你的生意伙伴 Rosy 的生日。请写信向她表示由衷的生日祝福，并在信中提及会赠送生日礼物给她。

Letter of Sympathy/Condolence

Part I Warm-up Case Study

Fasten your belt! You can begin an exciting journey towards learning to write a letter of sympathy/condolence efficiently by reading the following sample letters. While studying the letters, you need to discuss their functions, components, types and writing styles. Finally, you are expected to explore the writing techniques on drafting a letter of sympathy/condolence in a professional way. Now let's come to the following samples.

Case 1 A Sample Letter of Sympathy

Dear Mr. Gosh,

We were very concerned to hear about the recent misfortune at your factory and hope nobody was injured.

We hope you will be able to get over the accident and recover soon and your factory can resume operations as soon as possible.

As a token of sympathy, we would like to contribute US $20,000 to the rebuilding of your company. Meanwhile, if there is anything we can be of help, please let us know.

Yours faithfully,

Case 2 A Sample Letter of Condolence

Dear Mr. Lim,

It was a great sorrow that I have received the news of the death of your general manager

> Mr. Lee. His passing must be a great loss to your company and his business associates.
>
> I had the honor and the pleasure to know Mr. Lee and always regarded him as a personal friend. I will miss the cooperation with him and his generous nature.
>
> I would like to express my deepest sympathies to you and to his family. If there is any need in the coming few weeks, I will be more than happy to help.
>
> Yours faithfully,

Have you got some ideas about how to write a letter of sympathy/condolence after studying the above samples? If so, you are expected to do a brief analysis of the above samples and write down the key points.

KEY POINTS HERE

_____
_____
_____
_____
_____
_____
_____

Part II Having a Clear Picture

I. Concept of Letter of Sympathy/Condolence

Letters of sympathy/condolence may be among the most difficult ones to write for there's no set pattern for writing these kinds of letters.

Letters of condolence are used only in the event of death; however, letters of sympathy can be used both for death and for the purpose of consoling people when they suffer misfortunes, e.g. illnesses, injuries, natural disasters. Actually, the contents of condolence and sympathy mainly depend on the specific situation and the relationship between the writer and the person he is writing to.

II. Components of Letters of Sympathy/Condolence

Generally speaking, you should always keep in mind the following three parts while writing a letter of sympathy/condolence: opening, body, and closing.

1. Opening

In the opening of such letters, you acknowledge the unhappy events first. It is a good way for you to express your sorrow briefly and directly or mention by name the person who died. You may also tell how you heard the news, if appropriate.

2. Body

Your expression of heartfelt concern and your offer to help are of the most importance for the body. In this part, you need to express your feelings of loss, dismay or grief. Besides, you should also offer your sympathy, thoughts, good wishes (for sympathy) or prayers (for condolences). In case you write a letter of condolence, you should mention some positive memories the deceased gave you; or you may mention the virtues, achievements for which the deceased will be remembered. And one thing for you to remember is never to write sentences like "He was too young to die!"

3. Closing

The expression of affection or best wishes for the future are included to the end of your letters of sympathy/condolence. For example, you may end your letter by saying "with deepest sympathy to you and all your family." or "I wish you a very speedy recovery."

III. Types of Letters of Sympathy/Condolence

Letters of sympathy/condolence are sent out mostly in the following cases, including:

(1) Letter of sympathy to those who are ill;

(2) Letter of sympathy to those who have been injured;

(3) Letter of sympathy to those who have suffered material loss;

(4) Letter of sympathy to those who have suffered natural disasters;

(5) Letter of condolence to one's client;

(6) Letter of condolence on the death of a business associate;

(7) Letter of condolence on the death of relative.

IV. Tips for Letters of Sympathy/Condolence Writing

(1) Effective letters of sympathy/condolence should be warm and friendly.

(2) A proper and cordial style is needed in writing the letters of sympathy.

(3) It is not advisable for you to ask about the cause and details when a letter is drafted.

Part III　Showing Your Talent Slightly

Now that you have had a clear picture of the components and types of letters of sympathy/condolence, you can fulfill the following situational task with the help of the Warm-up Case Study.

I. Situational Task

(1) You work in Thompson Co., Ltd. and have heard that Mr. Paulio's factory got fire and the assets of the whole factory were lost. Write a letter of sympathy to him on behalf of your company.

(2) As the manager of Thompson Co., Ltd., you learned of the death of your business associate Mr. Zhang, the chairman of First Company. Write a letter of condolence to Mr. Liu, assistant of Mr. Zhang, to express your heartfelt condolences and also convey your deepest sympathies to Mr. Zhang's family.

II. Do It Yourself

1. A Letter of Sympathy

Dear Mr. Paulio,

_____
_____
_____
_____
_____
_____
_____

Yours faithfully,

2. A Letter of Condolence

Dear Mr. Liu,

_____
_____
_____
_____
_____
_____
_____

Yours faithfully,

Part IV Opening the Treasure Box

I. Samples

Sample 1 Letter of Sympathy to Those Who are Ill (1)

Dear Mr. Johnson,

When I learned from your secretary the news that you have been hospitalized and have to undergo an operation, I was deeply concerned.

I trust that the treatment you are going to receive will be quite successful. All the colleagues in our department are eagerly awaiting your return to the company.

Please accept my best wishes for a very speedy recovery.

Sincerely yours,

Sample 2 Letter of Sympathy to Those Who Are Ill (2)

Dear Lucy,

I am extremely sorry to hear of your sickness. You've been on my mind constantly ever since you went to hospital. Everybody in our office misses you so much and we are all expecting your completely recovery soon.

I hope that you don't have to worry about your work. We will help you. Just take things easy, and then you will get a speedy recovery.

Sincerely yours,

Sample 3 Letter of Sympathy to Those Who Have Been Injured (1)

Dear Mr. Howell,

I was quite shocked to hear that you had been in a car crash on your way to office. But I was also grateful that your injuries were not worse and you are now progressing nicely.

You are in the hearts and minds of everyone in the company and our thoughts are with you. Everyone in our department is hoping for your quick and complete recovery.

I hope you will continue to make good progress.

Sincerely yours,

Sample 4 Letter of Sympathy to Those Who Have Been Injured (2)

Dear Maria,

I am terribly sorry to hear that you got your leg hurt in the accident. The only good thing is that I learned form your mother that your injury is not so serious and you will be out of hospital in a week.

A little package from Tommy and I will soon reach you. And we hope the novel in it will help you while away the time.

With good wishes for your swift recovery.

Yours faithfully,

Sample 5 Letter of Sympathy to Those Who Have Suffered Material Loss (1)

Dear Mr. Martin,

We are sorry to hear about the accident in your factory and it was terrible to learn that many of your assets were destroyed in the explosion.

We sincerely hope you will soon be able to get over the accident. As a token of our friendship, we would like to make a contribution of US $10,000 to help you rebuild your factory.

We wish you all good luck in resuming the operations of your factory.

Yours sincerely,

Sample 6 Letter of Sympathy to Those Who Have Suffered Material Loss (2)

Dear Jody,

We are very sorry to learn from yesterday's newspaper that a fire broke out in your block, and your house was leveled.

I deeply know how much the house meant to you and your husband. Please accept my heartfelt sympathy on it. I know you and your family are living temporarily with the Reads. As soon as you begin rebuilding, please do not hesitate to let me know. I am more than happy to help.

Hope you and your family will soon be back in your own home.

Sincerely yours,

Sample 7 Letter of Sympathy to Those Who Have Suffered Natural Disasters

Dear Mr. Latch,

I was sorry to hear of the recent flooding which severely damaged your own factory.

It is among the most terrible things for self-employed businesspeople. I wish you all good luck in getting things back to normal as soon as possible.

Though I will temporarily place orders elsewhere, please be assured that I will bring my business back to you as soon as you are ready. I really appreciate our cooperation these years and look forward to doing business with you again.

Sincerely yours,

Sample 8 Letter of Condolence to One's Client

Dear Mr. Chou,

It was with great sorrow that we have received the news of the sudden death of your father.

There are no words to adequately express our sympathy for the profound loss you must be feeling. But all of us in China who have dealt with you would like you to know that you have our heartfelt sympathy.

Please accept our sincere condolences.

Sincerely yours,

Sample 9 Letter of Condolence on the Death of a Business Associate

Dear Mr. Reeve,

It came as a surprise to learn of Mr. Kent's death. I am writing at once to express my deepest condolences. His passing may mean a great loss to your company.

Mr. Kent and I are not only business associates, but also good friends for many years. He was admired by all of those who had business with him. Should there be anything I could help, just tell me. I will help out in any way I can.

Please convey my sincere condolences to his family.

Sincerely yours,

Sample 10 Letter of Condolence on the Death of One's Relative

Dear Mary,

  I feel deeply distressed to learn of the sad news of your brother and I hasten to offer my condolences.

  Though I haven't seen him since I left China, I have always remembered his disarming sense of humor and the pleasure of the wonderful days we spent together. I just want you to know that my thoughts are with you in this time of sorrow.

  Please accept my sympathy and convey my warm regards to your family.

Sincerely yours,

II. Related Expressions

(1) be hospitalized/be in hospital　　住院

　　be out of hospital　　出院

(2) get a speedy recovery　　早日痊愈

(3) I was quite shocked to hear that...　　获悉……感到非常震惊。

(4) be progressing nicely　　日渐好转

(5) Our thoughts are with you.　　我们无时不在惦记着你。

(6) while away the time　　消磨时间、打发时光

(7) It was terrible to learn that...　　听说……深感难过。

(8) hope you will soon be able to get over the accident

　　希望你能尽快从事故的痛苦中解脱出来

(9) make a contribution of US $10,000　　捐款一万美元

(10) resuming the operations　　恢复生产

(11) I am more than happy to help.　　我非常乐意提供帮助。

(12) Please be assured that...　　请放心……

(13) It was with great sorrow that I have received the news of the sudden death of...

　　获悉……突然去世的消息，我感到很难过。

(14) hasten to offer my condolences　　急表慰唁

III. Functional Sentences

(1) I am extremely sorry to hear of your illness.

　　听说你生病了，我感到非常不安。

(2) I can't tell you how sad I felt when I was informed of your unexpected illness.
当我获悉您突然得病时,我难过的心情真是难以诉说。

(3) I learned from your secretary the news that you have been in hospital.
从您秘书那里我得知您住院的消息。

(4) We were sad to know that you had to undergo an operation.
听说您要动手术,我们感到非常难过。

(5) I wish you a speedy and complete recovery.
祝你早日完全康复。

(6) With best wishes for your quick swift and complete return to health.
衷心祝您早日痊愈。

(7) I am eagerly awaiting your return to the company.
期待您康复,重返工作岗位。

(8) We just can't tell you how anxious we were to hear of your accident.
听说你出了车祸,不胜焦虑。

(9) If I can be of any help, please feel free to let me know.
如果我能帮上什么忙,请务必告诉我。

(10) I was deeply concerned to hear about the recent misfortune at your factory.
得知贵厂近来发生不幸事故,我深感不安。

(11) It was terrible to hear that many of your employees were injured in the accident.
得知贵厂很多员工在事故中受伤,我们很难过。

(12) We were shocked by the news of the big explosion in your factory and hope nobody was injured.
我们听说贵厂发生了大爆炸,深感震惊,希望没有人受伤。

(13) We just heard that due to the recent hurricane, your factory was severely damaged.
我方获悉,由飓风造成的灾害,使贵厂严重受损。

(14) I feel sorry indeed to have received the news of the death of your manager.
听到贵公司经理去世的消息我真的很难过。

(15) I was saddened to hear of your great loss.
得知你失去了亲人,我深感悲痛。

(16) It came as a surprise to learn of Mr. Liu's sad news.
惊悉刘先生去世的噩耗。

(17) I would like to be the one among those who share your sorrow at this sad time.
我愿在这个哀痛的时刻分担你的悲哀。

(18) My colleagues join me in conveying our sincere sympathy to members of his family.

我公司全体同仁及我向其家属表示由衷的慰问。

(19) Please accept our heartfelt sympathy.

请接受我们衷心的慰问。

(20) I would like to express my deepest sympathies to his family.

我愿向其家人表达我的深切慰问。

(21) Please convey my sincere condolences to all your family.

请转达我对你家人的真诚问候。

(22) Mr. Zhang was both loved and admired by all of his colleagues.

张先生深受同事的喜爱和尊敬。

(23) I would like to extend my deepest condolences to you at this time of great sorrow.

在此悲痛的时候，我谨向您表示我最深切的哀悼。

Part V Displaying Your Prowess Fully

I. Draft a letter of sympathy showing your consolation to the sick according to the hints given below in Chinese.

你从公司营销部经理林先生的秘书那里得知林先生卧病在床。请写信向其表示问候，祝他早日康复，并期待他在不久后就能回到公司上班。

II. Draft a letter of sympathy showing your consolation to the injured according to the hints given below in Chinese.

你的好友 Tommy 在公司组织的篮球比赛中受伤。请写一封慰问信，向他表达你的关心和良好的祝愿。

III. Draft a letter of sympathy showing your consolation to your business associate whose factory had been destroyed by the hurricane according to the hints given below in Chinese.

你从星球日报 (*Daily Planet*) 上得知你的生意伙伴 Mr. Adams 的工厂遭到飓风袭击毁于一旦。请写信表示慰问，并表示愿意捐款以示友谊和同情。并向其表达希望该厂能尽快恢复生产的良好祝愿。

IV. Fill in the blanks with the appropriate given expressions from a to e to complete the following letter.

Dear Mr. Wu,

We were ___(1)___ to learn about the misfortune at your company. We understand that it can't be a ___(2)___ for such an incident to happen.

It is our hope that ___(3)___ in this incident. If you need any help, just let us know. I could ___(4)___ some of my staff to help clear up the mess.

Hope everything will be ___(5)___ as soon as possible.

Sincerely yours,

a. there were no casualties

b. in order

c. very convenient time

d. send over

e. shocked

V. Draft a letter of condolence according to the hints given below in Chinese.

你获悉你的客户 Mr. Read 的儿子不幸病逝。请写信表示悼唁。

VI. The sentences below are mixed. Please separate and rearrange them to form a letter of sympathy and a letter of condolence.

(1) I know the suddenness of it must have been a dreadful shock.

(2) Please accept my heartfelt condolences and convey my deepest sympathies to your family.

(3) I feel very sorry to hear that.

(4) It came as a surprise to learn of your mother's sad news.

(5) I beg you to let me help you in any way I can.

(6) Just take things easy and you will get a swift recovery.

(7) It is good that your injury is not so serious and you will be back in a few days.

(8) The word of your accident just came to me this morning.

Letter of sympathy: _____

Letter of condolence: _____

Complaints and Replies

Part I Warm-up Case Study

Fasten your belt! You can begin an exciting journey towards learning to write a letter of complaint and its reply efficiently by reading the following sample letters. While studying the letters, you need to discuss their functions, components, types and writing styles. Finally, you are expected to explore the writing techniques on drafting a letter of complaint and its reply in a professional way. Now let's come to the following samples.

Case 1 A Sample Letter of Complaint

Dear Sirs,

The furniture that we bought on September 10 came this morning. However, upon examination, we found that the surface of the bookshelf was scratched badly.

It is in such a bad condition that we can hardly accept it. The scratch severely affects the beauty of the whole set of the furniture. Therefore, we would appreciate it if you will send a new one to me to replace the damaged one.

We hope you will put the matter right at once and we look forward to hearing from you.

Yours faithfully,

Case 2 A Sample Reply to the Above Letter

Dear Mr. Liu,

We have received your letter of September 18 regarding the damaged bookshelf.

We have investigated the matter and have found that the bookshelf had been damaged before making delivery. Such being the case, we agree to replace it. And we have already dispatched the replacement this morning.

We do apologize to you for the inconvenience you have suffered and we will make sure that this kind of incident will never happen again.

Yours faithfully,

Have you got some ideas about how to write a letter of complaint and its reply after studying the above samples? If so, you are expected to do a brief analysis of the above samples and write down the key points.

KEY POINTS HERE

_____
_____
_____
_____
_____
_____
_____
_____

Part II Having a Clear Picture

I. Concept of Complaints and Replies

No matter how well-planned and careful a business firm is, mistakes may happen and complaints will arise. As a customer, you may receive wrong goods, poor service, faulty products, etc. Therefore, letters of complaint, also called claims, are very common in daily life.

The replies to complaints are also called adjustment letters. The adjustment letters will help you keep goodwill of the complainant towards your company and sometimes give you the chance to win the customer back.

II. Components of Complaints and Replies

Generally speaking, you should always keep in mind the following three parts while writing complaints and replies: opening, body, and closing.

1. Opening

For the complaints, the opening part states the problem and gives as much information as possible. You should state the problem directly, when you noticed it and how it inconvenienced you. While for the replies, it is good for you to begin with a positive statement. Thank your customer for informing you.

2. Body

The body gives additional information for complaints. You should politely tell why it is important to resolve your problem and state what you expect from the company, such as repair, refund or replacement. If necessary, you may also suggest a deadline for the action. For the replies, you have to let your customer know how you will resolve the problem or what is being done. Sometimes, you have to give customers the choice of a replacement or a refund. However, if you find the complaint is unjustified, your reply should also be polite but firm.

3. Closing

For the complaints, in the closing part you should express your confidence politely that the company will solve the problem to their satisfaction. Threats and accusations will be annoying and make things worse. The closing for the replies reaffirms your company's good intentions. It is better to end your letter with the promise that this kind of error will rarely occur again to restore the confidence of your customers.

III. Types of Complaints

Letters of complaint can be used in the following situations, including:

(1) Letter of complaint for poor packing;

(2) Letter of complaint for damaged goods;

(3) Letter of complaint for non-delivery;

(4) Letter of complaint for short delivery;

(5) Letter of complaint for wrong goods;

(6) Letter of complaint for poor quality.

IV. Tips for Complaints and Replies Writing

(1) It is advisable for you to tell the truth in a more tactful way in making a complaint.

(2) Lay more emphasis on how the problem can be resolved in the letters of complaint.

(3) Respond to the complaints promptly so as to establish your good intentions.

(4) When replying, be specific about the actions you will take.

Part III Showing Your Talent Slightly

Now that you have had a clear picture of the components and types of complaints and replies, you can fulfill the following situational task with the help of the Warm-up Case Study.

I. Situational Task

(1) Suppose you are Mr. Lin and you have just received the new washing machine from the James Store. However, you found it was broken at the edge. Write a letter of complaint about this matter.

(2) Write a reply to the above letter, granting your adjustment.

II. Do It Yourself

1. A Letter of Complaint

Dear Sirs,

_____

_____

_____

_____

_____

_____

Yours faithfully,

2. A Reply to the Above

Dear Mr. Lin,

_____

_____

_____

_____

_____

_____

Yours faithfully,

Part IV Opening the Treasure Box

I. Samples

Sample 1 Letter of Complaint for Poor Packing

Dear Mr. Black,

We are writing to complain about the shipment of carpets under our Order No. 234.

When we took delivery of the carpets, we noticed some damage to the cases. The outer edges of the cases have been worn through and the carpets were soiled. It seems that the carpets were not packed properly before dispatch. Please let us know what you intend to do in this matter.

We are looking forward to hearing from you soon.

Sincerely yours,

Sample 2 A Reply to the Complaint for Poor Packing

Dear Mr. Brown,

We have received your letter dated November 11 regarding the damage of the carpets. Thank you for bringing the matter to our attention.

We are now making every effort to find the cause of the damage and we will report back our investigation results to you as soon as they are available.

Sincerely yours,

Sample 3 Letter of Complaint for Damaged Goods

Dear Mr. Bond,

The shipment of 200 boxes of glass wares arrived here yesterday. However, at the time of inspection, we found two boxes of glass wares were broken into pieces.

It looked as if they had been broken in transit. You will find enclosed a list of the damaged pieces and photographs made by our inspector. We suggest you replace two boxes of glass wares as soon as possible.

We look forward to your reply the soonest possible.

Sincerely yours,

Sample 4 A Reply to the Complaint for Damaged Goods

Dear Mr. Chen,

We thank you for calling attention in your letter of March 8, to the fact that the glass wares were damaged.

We have already investigated the matter carefully and have come to the conclusion that the two boxes of glass wares had been damaged before shipment. Therefore, we agree to send you another two boxes of glass wares as replacements. We will dispatch the replacements by airfreight in two days.

We apologize for the inconvenience we have been caused. We can assure you that in future we shall do all we can to avoid this error occurring again.

Yours faithfully,

Sample 5 Letter of Complaint for Non-delivery

Dear Sirs,

We would like to draw your attention to the order we placed with you for DSN camera on March 5. You stated that you would be able to deliver the goods in April, but we have been waiting for two months and we have still not received them.

We would like to remind you that we have already paid for these cameras. Therefore, we insist that you deliver them immediately or refund our money.

We should appreciate your looking into this matter and we await your favorable reply.

Yours sincerely,

Sample 6 Letter of Complaint for Short Delivery

Dear Sirs,

The cargo of 50 cases of typewriters has duly arrived. However, we feel it regrettable to find that the goods were short by 5 units in case No. 10.

We are in urgent need of these items as we have only a few stocks. In fact, our customers are pressing us for a timely delivery. Therefore, we shall be obliged if you will inquire into the matter and ship the five typewriters immediately upon receipt of this letter.

Thank you for your cooperation in advance.

Sincerely yours,

Sample 7 A Reply to the Complaint for Short Delivery

Dear Mr. Zhang,

We have received your letter of October 20 relating to the short delivery of 5 typewriters.

We have investigated the matter at our end and have found that the shortage is due to the carelessness of our stevedores. We will soon send you another 5 typewriters by airfreight.

Please accept our sincere apologies for the mistake in delivery, which may have caused inconvenience to you. We assure you of our best services for the future transactions.

Sincerely yours,

Sample 8 Letter of Complaint for Wrong Goods

Dear Mr. Toda,

We are writing in connection with our Order No. 123 for 1000 sets of TDF scanner. Unfortunately, you have sent us the wrong items. We ordered Model 802 but you have sent us the older Model 602.

We have already got many orders in advance from our customers which we must postpone because of this. It has caused us a great deal of inconvenience.

We should appreciate it if you would replace the goods you delivered with the correct ones.

We look forward to hearing from you soon.

Sincerely yours,

Sample 9 Letter of Complaint for Poor Quality

Dear Mr. Tong,

We are writing with reference to Order No. AF 501 for 1500 sets of photocopiers which we received yesterday.

Upon checking, we discovered that the photocopier do not function properly. They just fall far below the standard we expect. We have already got many orders from the end-users at our end. But now we have nothing to do but postpone the delivery. This will cause us a great deal of inconvenience.

We should like you to refund the money we have paid you for the photocopiers.

We look forward to hearing from you in the very near future.

Sincerely yours,

Sample 10 A Reply to the Complaint for Poor Quality

Dear Mr. Yang,

We refer to your letter of May 5 regarding the photocopiers we supplied to you.

Our sales representative Miss Zhao says that you checked the photocopiers very carefully before you make the decision to purchase and were aware of the standard of the workmanship.

Therefore, we regret to say that we cannot give you a refund because our goods are of saleable quality.

In view of our friendly relationship, we are prepared to offer you the more advanced ones at a considerably favorable price provided that you return the previous sets of photocopiers in good condition.

If this arrangement is acceptable to you, please contact us as soon as possible.

Sincerely yours,

II. Related Expressions

(1) under our Order No. 234   我方第 234 号订单项下

(2) take delivery   提货

(3) Thank you for bringing the matter to our attention.
    感谢贵方提出有关事项使我们注意。

(4) the soonest possible   尽早

(5) assure you that...   向你方保证……

(6) draw your attention to   提请贵方注意

(7) look into this matter   调查此事

(8) await your favorable reply   静候佳音

(9) pressing us for a timely delivery   敦促我方及时交货

(10) caused us a great deal of inconvenience   给我方带来极大不便

(11) In view of our friendly relationship   鉴于我们的友谊

(12) provided that   倘若、假如

(13) in good condition　　完好无损

(14) be acceptable to you　　可以被你方所接受

(15) postpone the delivery　　延期发货

III. Functional Sentences

(1) On checking the machine, we discovered that it did not function.

经检查，我们发现机器不能正常运转。

(2) We regret to tell you that on inspection we found a number of defects in your products.

我方很遗憾地通知你方，在检查中我们发现贵公司的产品有许多缺陷。

(3) On opening the outer packing we learned that some of the goods were missing.

开启外包装时，我们发现有一些货物缺失。

(4) We have received 200 sets of dinner wares instead of 200 tea sets.

我方收到的是二百套餐具而不是二百套茶具。

(5) The goods we received on May 15 were found not to match our order.

我方发现5月15日收到的货物与我们的订单不符。

(6) We have still not received the goods which we ordered on January 1.

我方1月1日订购的货物，至今仍未收到。

(7) We must complain about the quality of the goods that you recently sent us.

对于贵方最近发送的货物的质量问题，我们不得不向您提出投诉。

(8) We regret to say that the quality of your soybeans is far low the standard stipulated in the contract.

我方很抱歉地说，贵方这批大豆质量低于合同中规定的标准。

(9) We have already got many orders in advance from our customers which we shall now have to postpone because of your inefficiency.

我们已收到客户的许多订单，但由于贵方效率欠佳，不得不延期执行。

(10) We should be obliged if you would replace the goods with the correct ones.

如果贵方能更换发错的货物，我方不胜感激。

(11) We should appreciate it if you would look into this matter and arrange for delivery as soon as possible.

如贵方能对此进行调查，并尽快安排发货，我方将不胜感激。

(12) We regret to say that unless you can arrange for delivery in three days, we shall be obliged to cancel the order.

如果贵方在三天后不能发货，我方只能遗憾地取消订单。

(13) We appreciate your bringing the matter to our attention.

感谢贵方提出此事使我们注意。

(14) Thank you very much for informing us of this matter.

非常感谢贵方告知我方这一事件。

(15) We are making every effort to find the cause of the shortage.

我方正尽一切努力查找短缺原因。

(16) We are investigating the incident and we will report back to you the result as soon as possible.

我们正在调查这一事件，并会尽快将调查结果反馈给贵方。

(17) The delay was owing to the heavy weather.

延误是由于恶劣天气造成的。

(18) We apologize for the inconvenience which has been caused by our carelessness.

由于我方的疏忽给贵方造成不便，对此我方深表歉意。

(19) Our records indicate that the goods left here in perfect condition.

我方记录表明货物离开我地时一切完好。

(20) We regret to inform you that we are not responsible for the damage which takes place at sea.

我方很遗憾，货物在海上受损，对此我方不承担任何责任。

(21) We shall endeavor to make sure this does not happen again.

我们竭力确保此类事情不再发生。

(22) In order to compensate you for the inconvenience, we are prepared to offer a discount of 20% on your next order.

为了补偿给贵方带去的麻烦，我方准备在贵方下次订货时给予20%的折扣。

(23) We will send you the replacement within the next three days.

我方将在三天之内发去替换产品。

(24) We shall be glad to learn that you will give our complaint a quick response and we can get a satisfactory settlement within half a month.

若贵方能对此次投诉给予快速回应并于半月内完成理赔，我方将不胜欣慰。

(25) We accept all responsibilities for this explosion accident and greatly regret for serious casualties and loss of properties caused.

我方承担此次爆炸事故的全部责任，并对事故造成的重大人员伤亡和财产损失深表遗憾。

Part V Displaying Your Prowess Fully

I. Draft a letter of complaint for poor quality according to the hints given below in Chinese.

你 (Dawson) 收到供货商发来的一批光盘（optical disks），然而经检验发现，多数光盘无法储存资料，完全失去使用价值。请写信给供货方经理周先生投诉此事，并要求对方采取行动解决。

II. Draft a reply to the above letter according to the hints given below in Chinese.

请针对以上这封信写一封回信，说明问题出在生产过程中，并承诺会尽快解决此事，并更换这批光盘。

III. Draft a letter of complaint for short delivery according to the hints given below in Chinese.

你收到 200 台激光打印机 (laser printer)，然而发现其中 20 台缺少连接线 (connection cords)。写信投诉此事，并要求对方立即采取补救措施。

IV. Rearrange the following sentences to compose the body of a letter of complaint.

(1) We are in urgent need of the laptops, and your slowness is causing a great deal of inconvenience.

(2) We have placed an order with you for 500 sets of laptops on February 15.

(3) However, it is now over two months since we placed the order and we are still waiting for the goods.

(4) We would like to draw your attention to the fact that when we discussed delivery date, you assured us that you could deliver by March 3.

(5) We really must insist that you deliver them immediately or refund our money.

V. Rearrange the following sentences to compose the body of a negative reply to an unjustified complaint.

(1) It is clear that the damage must have occurred in the transportation.

(2) Therefore, we are not responsible for the damage and would like to advise you to claim on the shipping company.

(3) We regret to learn from your letter of June 6 of the damage of the goods we sent to you.

(4) The clean B/L showed that the goods were in good condition when they left here.

(5) At any rate, we deeply regret about this incident and we shall be pleased to claim on the shipping company on your behalf if necessary.

VI. Draft a letter of complaint for wrong goods according to the hints given below.

你收到了一封客户的投诉信。经过核实，客户 (Mr. Jordan) 的投诉是正当合理的。由于工作人员的失误货物发错了。现在请写信回复。你的回信要包含以下两点内容。

1. The right goods have been dispatched by air freight and will arrive within a week.
2. You will give the customer a 10 percent discount on this order.

Business Visits and Itineraries

Part I Warm-up Case Study

Fasten your belt! You can begin an exciting journey towards learning to write a letter of invitation and an itinerary efficiently by reading the following samples. While studying the samples, you need to discuss their functions, components, types and writing styles. Finally, you are expected to explore the writing techniques on drafting a letter of invitation and an itinerary in a professional way. Now let's come to the samples.

Case 1 A Sample Letter of Invitation

Dear Mr. Hendelson,

You are kindly invited to the Symposium on New-Technology Computer which will be held from July 6 to 9, 2010 at the International Trade Center in Shanghai. After the Symposium, there will be a trip to New-Tech Industrial Zone.

The New-Technology Computer is our latest issued products. As your computer science is in the leading position of Asia, we deem that your country will be the biggest market in this region. We hope the product will arouse your interest.

We are looking forward to meeting you at the Symposium.

Sincerely yours,

Case 2 A Sample Itinerary for Business Visits

ITINERARY

FOR

James Trade Mission

August 6–9, 2010

New York to Beijing

Monday, August 6

4:00 p.m.	Arrive in Beijing by Flight QQ 462, met by Mr. Zhou Liang, reception officer of the foreign affairs office
4:15 p.m.	Leave by car for Crystal Palace Hotel
7:00 p.m.	Dinner at hotel with Mr. Deng (Manager) and Mr. Hu (Office Director)

Tuesday, August 7

9:00 a.m.	Meeting with Mr. Liu, the Sales Manager at Conference Room
12:00 noon	Lunch with company executives
2:00 p.m.	Group discussion
4:00 p.m.	Visit the production line and new models at Hai Bin Development Zone
7:30 p.m.	Peking Duck Dinner

Wednesday, August 8

10:00 a.m.	Sign the Letter of Intent at VIP room
10:30 a.m.	Leave by car for the Crystal Palace Hotel
12:00 noon	Lunch at hotel
2:00 p.m.	Sightseeing as desired
6:30 p.m.	Buffet dinner at Crystal Palace Hotel hosted by Mr. Wu, General Manager

Thursday, August 9

7:45 a.m.	Leave by car
8:45 a.m.	Arrive at Beijing International Airport
12:30 p.m.	Return to New York by American Airlines Flight TT 906

Have you got some ideas about how to write a letter of invitation and an itinerary after studying the above samples? If so, you are expected to do a brief analysis of the above samples and write down the key points.

KEY POINTS HERE

___

Part II Having a Clear Picture

I. Concept of Business Visit and Itinerary

In international trade, official and business visits are very important and necessary both for an individual businessman and for delegations. The people concerned have to make great preparations (including the exchange of letters) before they plan a visit to a foreign country or entertain a foreign delegation. The letters concerning business visits usually include visit proposals, invitations and thanks on return.

An itinerary is usually a plan of business visits, which includes the route, the places to be visited, etc. It is necessary for the host to prepare an effective itinerary while you receive an individual visitor or a delegation. In most cases, an itinerary is used as a reception plan in international activities, known as a program.

II. Components of Letters for Business Visits

Generally speaking, you should always keep in mind the following three parts while writing letters concerning business visits: opening, body, and closing.

1. Opening

In a visit proposal, the opening part directly states the intention of your visit. While drafting an invitation, you need to state the purpose of invitation in the first part. If you write a letter of reply, it is wise for you to briefly describe in this part the reason why you are writing the letter.

2. Body

The body of the visit proposals gives necessary information. You should state your purpose, name and position of the visitor and accompanying staff, and your designed time arrangements. In general, a letter of invitation usually gives the detailed information, for example, time, place, activities. However, you are expected to express your goodwill by making some personalized comments.

3. Closing

In closing a visit proposal, you should ask for a reply whether your proposed time is agreeable or not, and also express your wish to receive a favorable reply. In the last part of an invitation, you'd better end with the hope that your invitation can be accepted. While closing a letter of reply, you need repeat your appreciation in a way different from the opening.

III. The Layout of Itineraries

In order to have an eye-catching effect, itineraries are usually neatly laid out, which usually include the following parts:

(1) Headline;

(2) Duration of visit;

(3) Places to visit;

(4) Planned activities.

To make them clear, all these usually break into several lines.

IV. Types of Letters for Business Visits

Letters concerning business visits usually include the following:

(1) Letters of visit proposal;

(2) Letters of invitation;

(3) Letters of thanks on return.

V. Tips for Business Visits and Itineraries Writing

(1) A letter concerning business visits should be sincere but not too long.

(2) An itinerary should usually include headline, time, places and activities.

(3) For the purpose of conciseness, the details of planned activities are presented with noun and verb phrases instead of full sentences.

Part III Showing Your Talent Slightly

Now that you have had a clear picture of the components and types of letters concerning business visits and itineraries, you can fulfill the following situational tasks with the help of the Warm-up Case Study.

I. Situational Task

(1) Write a letter to a British firm, inviting them to take part in the International Fair that

will be held from October 10 to 25, 2018 in Beijing.

(2) Please prepare an itinerary for the guests of the British Trade Delegation, who will visit your city in August. The itinerary should include details as to where to stay, what to do, whom to meet, and places to visit.

II. Do It Yourself

1. A Letter of Invitation

Dear Sirs,

_____
_____
_____
_____
_____
_____
_____
_____
_____
_____
_____
_____

Yours faithfully,

2. An Itinerary

<u>ITINERARY</u>
<u>FOR</u>
<u>BRITISH TRADE DELEGATION</u>

_____
_____
_____
_____
_____
_____
_____
_____
_____
_____
_____
_____

Part IV Opening the Treasure Box

I. Samples

Sample 1 A Letter of Visit Proposal (1)

Dear Sirs,

We take the pleasure in advising that our Export Manager, Mr. Kwok wishes to visit your country in May of this year for the purpose of entering into business relations with your manufacturers of porcelain wares for importation to Britain. Therefore, we should appreciate it if you would furnish us with an invitation to the Canton Fair.

We are looking forward to hearing from you soon.

Sincerely yours,

Sample 2 A Letter of Visit Proposal (2)

Dear Sirs,

We have the pleasure to inform you that Mr. Jason Kent, our Minister and his accompanying delegation would like to visit Beijing to continue our business negotiation. They plan to leave in the first half of June and remain in Beijing for about 10 days.

We would be grateful to be informed as soon as possible whether this planned visit is convenient for you and what itinerary you would suggest.

Sincerely yours,

Sample 3 A Letter of Invitation (1)

Dear Mr./Ms.,

We would like to invite you to attend the International Fair which will be held from September 25 to October 5 at the International Exposition Center in Tianjin. Full details on the Fair will be sent to you in a week.

As one of our distinguished customers, we would like you to attend the Fair. We look forward to your presence.

Yours faithfully,

Sample 4 A Letter of Invitation (2)

Dear Sirs,

We would like to invite your corporation to attend the Sino-US Agricultural Products Trade Exhibition to be held from September 20 to 24 in Beijing. We look forward to welcoming you to this exhibition where your products will be best displayed. Full details on the Exhibition will be airmailed to you in three days.

We hope you will be able to accept this invitation.

Yours faithfully,

Sample 5 A Letter of Thanks on Return (1)

Dear Mr. Beckham,

Thank you very much for your hospitality when my accompanying delegation and I were in Washington.

I am writing to express my thanks for your arranging such an excellent program for us. I really appreciate the business contacts you introduced and the information you brought us. I am confident that on a foundation of mutual trust, we will be able to develop trade cooperation between us on a substantial and beneficial scale.

Again, many thanks to your hospitality!

Yours sincerely,

Sample 6 A Letter of Thanks on Return (2)

Dear Mr. Howard,

Now that I am back in Beijing, I am writing to say how pleased I was to be able to meet you during my visit to Australia.

I really appreciate your help during my visit to your company.

I would like to offer you any similar service in the future when you pay a visit to our company. Please feel free to contact me.

Thanks for your warm hospitality once again.

Sincerely yours,

Sample 7 An Itinerary

ITINERARY

FOR

Mr. Blake, the Sales Director of Aston Company

October 5–8, 2010

Xi'an

Tuesday, October 5

4:40 p.m.	Arrive at Xi'an Xianyang International Airport by Flight MC 1581, met by Miss Chen, staff of Foreing Affairs Office
5:10 p.m.	Arrive at Shangri-la Hotel and check in
6:30 p.m.	Leave by car for Kempinski Hotel
7:00 p.m.	Reception given by the President of Jk Co., Ltd. at Kempinski Hotel

Wednesday, October 6

8:00 a.m.	Leave the Shangri-la Hotel for the headquarter of Jk Co., Ltd.
8:30 a.m.	Business talks
10:30 a.m.	Appointment with General Manager
11:30 a.m.	Lunch at International Club
2:00 p.m.	Visit Hi-tech Industrial Park, accompained by Sales Manager

Thursday, October 7

8:00 a.m.	Sightseeing to the Huaqing Pool
11:30 a.m.	Lunch at Huaqing Pool
1:00 p.m.	Leave by car for the Museum of the Terra-cotta Warriors and Horses of Qin Shihuang
3:00 p.m.	Back to Xi'an, Jianhua Shopping Center (1.5 hours' stay)
Evening	Free from engagements

Friday, October 8

8:00 a.m.	Check out at Shangri-la Hotel
8:45 a.m.	Leave by car for Xi'an Xianyang International Airport
10:50 a.m.	Departure for Beijing

II. Related Expressions

(1) We take the pleasure in advising that   我们高兴地通知贵方

(2) enter into business relations with　与……建立业务关系

(3) furnish sb. with...　向某人提供……

(4) accompanying delegation　×××所率代表团

(5) You are kindly invited to...　特邀贵方到……

(6) in the leading position　处于领先地位

(7) arouse your interest　引起贵方的兴趣

(8) Full details on the Exhibition will be airmailed to you in three days.
全部详细资料将于三天内发出。

(9) Thank you very much for your hospitality.　感谢您的盛情款待。

(10) on a foundation of mutual trust　在相互信任的基础上

(11) We will be able to develop trade cooperation between us on a substantial and beneficial scale.
我们之间在贸易上的协作将在对双方互利的情况下长足发展。

(12) Reception given by the President of Jk Co., Ltd. at Kempinski Hotel.
JK有限公司董事长在凯宾斯基酒店举行的宴会。

(13) business talks　商务会谈

(14) Visit... , accompanied by...　由……陪同参观……

(15) Free from engagements　自由活动

(16) Departure for Beijing　乘航班赴北京

III. Functional Sentences

(1) We take the pleasure to inform you that our Director proposes that his delegation arrive in Guangzhou on Monday, February 15, remain in Guangzhou for four days for business negotiation.
兹函告，我方主管建议我代表团于2月15日（星期一）抵达广州，在广州停留四日，进行业务谈判。

(2) We should appreciate it if you could inform us as soon as possible whether the planned visit would be convenient.
如能尽快答复上述访问计划对贵方是否合适，我方不胜感激。

(3) Please let us know if the planned visit is convenient for you and what itinerary you would suggest.
请告知上述访问计划是否合适，以及你方建议的访问日程表。

(4) We have the pleasure of informing you that our Sales Manager, Mr. Denken wishes to visit your country in May in order to seek business opportunity.
我们高兴地通知贵方，我公司销售部经理邓肯先生拟于5月访问贵国，以寻求商机。

(5) We look forward to welcoming you to our company and discussing with you our latest developments in Machinery Manufacture Industry.
我方非常欢迎您来我公司访问，并愿就我方机械制造业最新发展事宜同您进行商谈。

(6) We are looking forward to an early opportunity of discussing the relevant matters with you.
殷切盼望有机会尽早与您商讨相关事宜。

(7) We should invite you to attend the Canton Fair to be held from April 15 to 20.
兹邀请贵公司参加4月15日至4月20日举行的广交会。

(8) We look forward to hearing from you soon, and hope you will be able to attend.
期盼早日收到贵方答复，并希望您能与会。

(9) We would like to invite you to our new custom-built factory premises in Shenzhen.
我方想邀请您来深圳参观我们特别定制的新建厂房。

(10) You are invited to attend the Symposium on "International Cooperation in Investment in the 21st Century" on December 20 to 28, 2010.
特邀您参加2010年12月20日至28日举行的"21世纪国际投资合作高级研讨会"。

(11) The Seminar will be run at the International Conference & Exhibition Centre. Refreshments will be provided throughout the day.
研讨会将在国际会展中心举行。会议期间有茶点招待。

(12) Please apply for your visa at the nearest Chinese Embassy with this invitation letter.
请凭此邀请函就近向中国大使馆申请签证。

(13) We look forward to your presence. Just call our office and we will be glad to secure the place for you.
期待您的光临。只需拨打我们办公室电话，我们非常愿意为您保留位子。

(14) Back now in my own country I wish to thank you for your hospitality extended to me.
我已平安返国，对您给予的热情款待谨表感谢。

(15) I am writing to express my gratitude for your help during my visit to your company.
谨以此信表达对您的感谢之情，在我访问贵公司期间，您提供了莫大的帮助。

(16) I found all the meetings and visits very interesting indeed.
贵方安排的所有会晤和参观项目都确实令人感到振奋。

(17) Thank you for your hospitality which helped make my visit to Paris particularly memorable.
您的热情款待使我访问巴黎之行特别令人难忘，对此谨表谢意。

(18) The opportunity to meet you and your delegation is something I had long looked forward to.
与您及所率代表团会晤是我早已向往之事。

(19) I can only hope now that some day I may be able to receive a visit here from you.
我现在只希望有一天可以迎接贵方莅临本地。

(20) Leave Beijing International Airport for London
离开首都国际机场飞赴伦敦

(21) Met by Mr. Louise and transferred to Astor Hotel
由路易斯先生接机，并送至阿斯特酒店下榻

(22) Dinner at hotel　在宾馆用晚餐

(23) Meeting with Manager of Imp./Exp. Department
与进出口部经理会谈

Part V　Displaying Your Prowess Fully

I. Draft a letter of visit proposal according to the hints given below in Chinese.

请代表英国某公司的业务主管向广州纺织品公司写一封访问建议信，并希望对方提供春季广交会请帖。

II. Draft a letter of invitation according to the hints given below in Chinese.

请写信邀请马可公司进出口部经理卡梅隆先生参加你公司影像设备（audio-visual equipment）新产品展示会，并表示可以提供接机服务。

III. Draft a letter of thanks on return according to the hints given below in Chinese.

你所率领的商务访问团已返回天津。请写信向芝加哥贸易公司贸易部官员的热情款待表示谢意，并希望能在不久后在天津再次与对方会晤。

IV. Draft an itinerary according to the following Chinese.

比利时贸易代表团访问北京活动日程
9月7日至9月9日
北京

9月7日（星期二）

　　　　上午9时　　抵达北京，由悦华公司贸易代表刘先生在机场迎接

　　　　上午9时15分　　乘车前往希尔顿酒店下榻

　　　　上午11时45分　　在酒店用午餐

下午 2 时　　拜会悦华公司总经理

　　下午 3 时　　与进出口部经理会谈

　　下午 7 时　　出席悦华公司总经理在希尔顿酒店举行的宴会

9 月 8 日（星期三）

　　上午 9 时　　继续前一日与进出口部经理的业务磋商

　　上午 11 时 30 分　　午餐

　　下午 1 时 30 分　　乘车参观悦华公司新技术产业园，由进出口部经理陪同

　　下午 6 时 30 分　　出席使馆招待会

9 月 9 日（星期四）

　　上午 7 时 30 分　　前往长城游览

　　上午 11 时 30 分　　在长城用午餐

　　下午 2 时　　返回北京，前往西单国际购物中心购物

　　晚间　　自由活动

Fundamentals of Business Writing

Basic Requirements for Business Writing

Part I Having a Clear Picture

I. Functions of Business Writing

As international business and trade activities are rapidly increasing, business writing becomes more and more significant. Normally, business texts perform three functions: to inform, to influence and to entertain. Messages are designed to convey the vast amount of information needed to complete the day-to-day operation of the business – to explain instructions to employees, announce meeting and giving responses to request letters, place orders, or make complaints, accept contracts for services, etc. Apart from providing information, a business text is used to influence readers' attitudes and actions. These messages might include sales letters for promoting products or services and seeking support for ideas and worthy causes presented to supervisors, stockholders, customers or clients. There are also other messages prepared to entertain them, that is, to establish good relationships with them and/or convey goodwill to them. Many business texts combine two or three functions. In short, business texts are used to keep business going smoothly, efficiently and productively.

II. Principles of Business Writing

There are certain essential qualities of business messages, which can be summed up in the seven C's, namely, Courtesy, Conciseness, Clarity, Completeness, Correctness, Concreteness, Consideration.

1. Courtesy

The principle of courtesy means using tactful, respectful and appreciative words or expressions in writing a text to show your respect for the readers. Courtesy plays an important role in business correspondence. It can help build a good image of your company and deepen the business relationship. So it is necessary to avoid hurting expression and you should select some polite and tactful words.

For example:

(1) *Thank you for* your letter of March 4, 2018.

(2) *Please* let us know at once if you need some other information.

(3) *Please accept our hearty thanks for your kind invitation* to your marriage on Friday, January 12, at two o'clock in the afternoon.

2. Conciseness

It means to write the fewest useful words without losing essential elements. Effective writing is concise about each word, sentence and paragraph as a busy reader will not waste any unnecessary time. Try to keep your sentences short, avoid unnecessary repetition and eliminate excessive details.

For example:

(1) In addition, we are *also* including a current price list.

　　In addition, we are including a current price list. (improved)

(2) I came back *because of the fact that* I had forgotten to take my books.

　　I came back because I had forgotten to take my books. (improved)

(3) The *workers who produce the most* will receive bonuses.

　　The most productive workers will receive the bonuses. (improved)

(4) The *tendency of those who are old is* to avoid situations that are new and unfamiliar.

　　The old tend to avoid unfamiliar situations. (improved)

3. Clarity

Clarity refers to making the information clear so that the readers can understand what you are going to convey. It tells the readers exactly what they want to know, using short, familiar words and sentences rather than long, complex and difficult ones. And a writer is supposed to organize effective sentences and paragraphs.

Compare the following sentences:

(1) I am writing to apply for admission to your university.

　　I am writing to apply for admission to the graduate school of your university in the spring of 2004. (improved)

(2) Packed in a box, the typist could not find the machine.

　　Packed in a box, the machine could not be found. (improved)

4. Completeness

Business writing should include all the necessary information and data. A complex message may bring you hoped-for results, establishment of goodwill. On the contrary, an incomplete one may head to increased communication costs, loss of valued customers, cost of returning goods, etc. Whether the business writing is complete or not, we may use 5 "Ws" to check—who, what, when, where and why or how.

5. Correctness

Correct grammar, punctuation and spelling are basically required in business writing. In addition, correctness means choosing the correct level of language, and using accurate information and data.

For example:

It is said in China Daily that the fourth World Conference on Women will be held in Beijing in September, 1995.

6. Concreteness

Business writing should be vivid, specific and definite especially when you are requiring something. We should certainly manage to be concrete in business writing, but sometimes we conscientiously avoid some details for civilities.

Compare the following examples to see which one is more appropriate:

(1) We wish to confirm our telegram *yesterday*.

We confirm our telegram of March 29, 2018. (improved)

(2) We have received with thanks *your check*. The amount has been placed to your credit.

We have received with thanks *your check No. 23 for us, in payment of our machines*. The amount has been placed to your credit. (improved)

7. Consideration

Skillful business writers always visualize their readers' needs, problems, customs and reactions to the writing and put themselves in the readers' position. In addition, it is necessary to consider the readers' sex, and level of education, etc.

Compare the following examples:

(1) Congratulations to you on your.... (*you–attitude*)

We want to send our congratulations... (*we–attitude*)

(2) As mentioned in our June 18 letter to you... (*tactful*)

Obviously you have forgotten what I wrote to you three years ago. (*blunt*)

III. Language Skills in Business Writing

1. Comparing

(1) Comparison of equivalence: as...as, the same as, as much of...as, identical with, similar to, etc.

Our competitor produces *as many models as* we do.

As much of capital is raised at home as a broad.

I agree with you *as much as* Mr. Robert.

Our product is *identical* in specifications *with* the Japanese make.

The turnover of the company in the second quarter remained *the same as* that of the corresponding period last year.

Our views are not quite *similar to* those of our trading partners.

(2) Comparative and superlative degree

The quality of our products is *much better than* that of competing ones.

This is *the most competitive* market in the whole world.

The conditions imposed on us are *even less* acceptable.

The bigger the project, *the higher* the cost.

The facts speak *louder than* words.

(3) Other forms: superior to, inferior to, over, beyond, so that, such that, too, enough, exceed, surpass, etc.

The home-made machine is *superior to* the imported one in many aspects.

In the first half of 1988 the monthly deficits consistently *exceeded* $2 billion mark.

It is not advisable to live *beyond* one's means.

He is experienced *enough* to understand the trap.

It moves *too* quickly for most people *to* see.

It is flying *so fast that* it may beat the speed record.

It is *such* a good chance *that* we mustn't miss it.

2. Cause and Effect: because of, owing to, due to, cause, lead to, result in, be caused by, result from, be attributed/attributable to, etc.

The failure of the Suggestion Scheme is *due to* the low reward.

The American measures *led to* immediate reaction from the world.

Owing to our joint efforts, the transaction was successfully concluded.

Ineffective management *caused/resulted in* poor profits.

The collapse of the company *was caused/resulted from* a strategic mistake by the president.

The delivery was delayed *because of* rough weather.

3. Condition: if

If the junior recruiters work more than four hours overtime, they receive overtime payments.

If business starts to improve, salaries will be increased.

If Site A were chosen, 30 square meters of parking space would be lost.

If the increase had been more moderate, profitability would have kept pace with the rise in turnover.

4. Contrast: although, even though, whereas, while, however, etc.

Turnover increased. *However*, profitability fell.

Although turnover increased, profitability fell.

Profitability fell *even though* turnover increased.

It would be difficult to ventilate Site B, *while/whereas* the exterior position of Site A would improve ventilation.

While I know the good opportunity in the proposed investment, I fully realize the risks that may be involved in it.

5. Example: for example, for instance, such as, like, or, etc.

The British fleet prevented Germany from importing *such* essentials *as* foodstuffs, petroleum, cotton, rubber, and tin, so necessary in the work of war.

In a friendship *such as* ours a few slips are of no consequence.

Some trade unions, the Electrical Trades Union, *for example*, gave us their full support in the labor dispute.

The world needs international economic bodies *like* World Trade Organization to regulate the economic and trade development.

6. Sequence: first, second(ly), last, before, after, another, next, then, afterwards, later on, finally, followed by, preceded by, etc.

The following is a description of how paper is made. *First*, the logs are put in the shredder(切碎机). *Then* they are cut into small chips and mixed with water and acid. Next they are heated and crushed to a heavy pulp to be cleaned. It is also chemically bleached to whiten it. *After this*, it is passed through rollers to flatten it. *And then*, sheets of wet paper are produced. *Finally*, the water is removed from the sheets which are pressed, dried and refined until the finished paper is produced.

7. Similar Things: and, also, as well, as well as, moreover, furthermore, in addition, in addition to, besides, similarly, etc.

We agreed on the terms of payment in today's negotiation. *Besides* that, we *also* discussed other terms but more negotiations are still required before coming to an agreement on them.

The house is not big enough for us, *and furthermore*, it is too far away from the town.

In addition to advertising, the Marketing Manager is in charge of many other promotional activities.

Their full political rights, *as well as* their economic conditions, must be safeguarded.

8. Summarizing: in short, in brief, in a word, in summary, in conclusion, briefly, to summarize, to sum up, to conclude, etc.

The above-mentioned two points are the official view, *in brief*, of the trade union on the current issue.

To summarize, we are unable to accept your conditions but agree to continue our negotiation after consulting the home office.

The troubled enterprise, *in short*, must be reformed and reorganized for a turnaround.

Briefly, the overseas operation of the multinational company has proved to be a great success.

IV. Writing Techniques

1. Composition

As is known to all, composition is to describe the relationship between the whole and the parts.

(1) Main and sub parts: be made up of, consist of, include, can be/be broken down into, can be/be divided into, can be/be separated into, etc.

The Personnel Department *is divided into* five sections.

One section, Training, *consists of* ten staff.

(2) Hierarchical structure: above/below, over/under, on the same level, at the top, at the bottom, headed by, etc.

The Division *is headed by* an Executive Director. *Below* him, there are three line managers.

(3) Additional parts: besides, in addition to, also, not only...but also, etc.

There are six other directors on the board *in addition to* the Managing Director.

2. Impersonal Reporting

Generally speaking, the first person is linked with something informal, while impersonal reporting is used with something formal or important.

(1) Opinion

... *is discussed*.

... *is considered*.

It is felt that...

Opinion varies about...

Different opinions are expressed about...

(2) Agreement/disagreement

It is agreed that...

There is no agreement about...

(3) Recommendation

It is suggested that...

It is recommended that...

It is proposed that...

(4) Conclusion

It is concluded that...

No conclusions are reached about...

It is decided that...

3. Classification

Classification is widely used in business writing, therefore it is very necessary to learn skills for classification. The following is a good example using classification approach.

Here is the report you requested on the costs involved in putting your slides in the existing file.

(1) *Software development*

(2) *Terminal lease*

(3) *Slide insertion*

(4) *Storage and use*

4. Fact and Opinion: in fact, as a matter of fact, actually; in my view, in my opinion, it seems to me, I feel (think, believe...) that... , etc.

In business writing, it is very important to distinguish facts and opinions as opinions are based on facts.

Many analysts *believe* that the U.S. economy will continue to grow for the next few months. (opinion)

Official statistics indicate the world commodity trade grew strongly last year. (fact)

The new plant *should* have been completed six months ago. (opinion). But *in fact*, what has been done is only a little more than half of its work. (fact) It *may* still need another year to complete.(opinion)

5. Inductive Approach

The inductive method starts with observations, and then makes analysis of the facts, finally comes to a few powerful statements about how it works. The following is a good example in terms of inductive approach.

Generally speaking, advertisements are constructive to both manufacturers and consumers. *With advertisements*, manufacturers and their products become more popular and consumers are better informed and given more choices. *However*, advertisements sometimes may become ridiculous or even deceiving. *For example*, one drug advertisement went as far as declaring that it is the absolute remedy for AIDS. Many consumers have complained of being taken in by such deceiving advertisements. Governments at all levels, *therefore*, should exercise more rigid examination of *advertisements* before they are exposed to the general public.

6. Deductive Approach

The deductive approach works from the more general to the more specific. Sometimes this is informally called a "top-down" approach. It begins with the statements and then offers the supporting details. Next is an example using the deductive approach.

For our particular needs, the most appropriate in-service training method is programmed instruction. *First of all*, it is least expensive. It *also* allows employees to remain at their work station while improving their skills, affords constant awareness of progress, and lets employees progress at their own rates.

Part II Displaying Your Prowess Fully

I. Try to improve the following sentences according to the principles of business writing.

(1) Please send me your catalogs on clothes.

(2) Consequent upon the changes made, you will be in charge of the financial department.

(3) Managers of all departments will meet at 9:30 on Monday.

(4) We have received your order of a large volume.

(5) In the event that we cannot meet the deadlines, we will refund your money.

(6) We have duly received your remittance dated March 11, for which please accept our thanks.

(7) This email is to inform you of an important change in our policy concerning transportation.

(8) You obviously made a mistake by sending us the wrong goods.

II. Complete the following sentences with the words and expressions given below.

(1) beyond understanding/too difficult/it is/and/the problem/is

(2) he makes/friends/the more/information/the more /he gets

(3) as good as/made in/they make/those/are/the trucks/Changchun

(4) the least/among/I am/experienced/the teachers here

(5) I don't agree/that the problem/they cannot be solved/the problem are difficult/while

(6) send us/if/another copy of/we will pay it/at once/you/your invoice

(7) to bring up/really not easy/such a single woman as/it is/for/Mrs. Green/five children

(8) some trade unions/gave us/for example/their full support/the Electrical Trades Union

III. Rearrange the following sentences into an effective paragraph.

(1) In step 2 the employer may ask you to complete a company application form. Not all the candidates can proceed to this step.

(2) Finally, only the most successful candidates will get an offer of employment.

(3) There are five steps in the job-seeking process.

(4) Then if you can go to the screening interview step, you should make the employer feel that you have a strong potential.

(5) The first step is to make initial contact by presenting yourself at the employer's door, by writing a letter, or by telephone.

(6) The employer will choose even fewer promising candidates to attend a second interview — the selection interview.

IV. Fill in the blanks with suitable transitional words.

(1) Our Accountants Receivable Department has written to you three times; _____, we have had no response to our letter.

(2) The bill of lading did not match the order; _____, the shipment was refused.

(3) Jeanette considered the possibility of changing a job _____ was unwilling to accept

the risks involved.

(4) Please place your order immediately, _____ you will not be eligible for the discount.

(5) Information concerning equipment used in business offices is needed; _____, we are conducting a survey.

(6) Members of our management staff, _____, are interested in hiring a consultant to train customer personnel.

(7) Our department is currently understaffed; _____, we are behind on our production schedule.

(8) Servco has produced, _____, a tool with remarkable safety features and excellent ease of handling.

V. Point out the sentences that do not develop the central idea.

Paragraph 1

(1) Strict measures should be taken to stop air pollution. (2) The government should pass laws to prevent factories and cars from sending out harmful gases into the air. (3) Those who violate the law should be severely punished. (4) In addition, every one who breaks the law should be punished, such as those who desert the families, those who violently beat women and children, and laws are the only way to control their behaviors. (5) With effective laws and policies of controlling air pollution, we believe the air in big cities will be clean and healthy.

Paragraph 2

(1) These energy resources are being used up rapidly. (2) We use energy to run our factories, run our cars and trains, and heat our homes. (3) Energy is becoming more and more expensive. (4) In a word, we have a great need for energy because of our economic growth and daily life.

Paragraph 3

(1) The invention and improvements of the computer has been a sudden process. (2) Computers were invented only a generation age. (3) The first ones were relatively slow and took a lot of space. (4) Thousands of computers are produced in USA. (5) Today, however, computers can fit into a briefcase and provide massive amounts of information in an instant.

Unit 20

Word-selecting and Sentence-making

Part I Having a Clear Picture

I. Selecting Words

The right words can communicate best and have correct meanings in readers' mind. How to select the right words depends on your ability in using language, your knowledge about readers and your good judgment.

1. Using Short and Familiar Words

Business writers choose short, familiar, and conversational words instead of long, unfamiliar ones.

Compare the following examples:

A. Long and unfamiliar words	B. Short and familiar words
domicile	home, house
utilize	use
for the reason that	since
due to the fact that	because
remuneration	pay
for the purpose of	for

2. Using Concrete Language

Concrete language is marked by the sharp and clear meanings in the readers' mind. Abstract wordings cover broad meanings, concepts, ideas and the like. They are vague and general.

Compare the following examples:

A. Abstract	B. Concrete
in the coming days	by Wednesday afternoon
the minority	15 percent
a significant loss	a 65 percent loss

3. Using Active Voice

Active voice makes writing stronger and livelier. It emphasizes taking action and usually expresses concisely. How to choose an appropriate voice depends on concrete situations. Passive voice is better especially when the performer is not known or not wanted to be mentioned, such as in the following examples:

(1) *In the last month, the exercises have been repeated there times.*

(2) *The conference will be held on Wednesday between 9:00 a.m. and 11:00 a.m.*

(3) *The letter was marked "confidential."*

(4) *We ordered the books two months ago.*

(5) *Seniors take courses just before graduation.*

(6) *The president delivered the address to the ABA last week.*

4. Selecting Words for Precise Meaning

Effective writing requires better knowledge of language. You will need to study English words carefully, especially the shades of difference in the meanings of similar words, if you want to be a good English writer. Abundant knowledge of language enables you to use words efficiently and accurately.

II. Joining of Sentences

1. Coordinating Conjunctions: and, or, but, nor, etc.

(1) We think your action is illogical, unfair *and* arbitrary.

(2) People can choose to communicate in international business by correspondence, telephone, *or* fax.

(3) Karen is interested in a job in marketing, *but* she wants to go abroad for further studies too.

2. Conjunctive Adverbs: nevertheless, however, consequently, therefore, thus, on the other hand, in the mean time, on the contrary, that is, accordingly, etc.

(1) Electricians rewired the equipment room; *nevertheless*, fuses continued to blow.

(2) Some machines require separate outlets; *consequently*, new outlets were installed.

(3) Complex equipment requires operators who are specialists; *thus* we must train operators to become specialists.

(4) Equipment expenditures are very great this quarter; *on the other hand*, new equipment will reduce labor costs.

(5) The foreign partner did not fulfill our order, *nor* did it intend to.

3. Correlative Conjunctions: both... and... , not only...but also... , either...or... , neither...nor... , etc.

(1) Your glasses are *either* on the counter *or* on the table.

(2) *Both* industry *and* agriculture are making great strides in the country.

(3) *Not only* was she gracious, *but also* she was kind.

(4) I have *neither* the time *nor* the energy for this.

4. Subordinating Conjunctions: before, after, when, while, until, unless, because, since, although, so that, that, whether... or... , if, as if/though, provided/providing, so long as, etc.

(1) Mr. Lee signs only his initials *when* he writes memos.

(2) *Since* Mrs. Sims works with customers, she writes many letters.

(3) We will ship the goods within the week, *if* that is satisfactory with you.

(4) *Before* they left the office, they finished the project.

5. Relative Pronouns: whom, who, whose, which, that, etc.

(1) The first orientation program, *which* begins on October 2, has already been filled.

(2) The German car *that/which* you bought two years ago is still worth $20,000.

(3) We are now seeking a bright young man *whom* we can train to take important positions.

(4) The contract, *whose* stipulations have been negotiated over the past six months, is to be signed this week.

6. Relative Adverbs or Conjunctions: when, where, why and how; if, whether, etc.

(1) The manager couldn't understand *why* they turned down the proposal.

(2) It is essential for you to definitely tell us *when* you are able to deliver the ordered goods.

(3) The new report is about *where* people have invested most and how they have invested.

(4) That depends on *whether* you will accept the plan or not.

(5) The board wanted to know *if* the company was performing well.

III. Effective Sentences

It is not difficult to write grammatical correct sentence, but a correct sentence is not always an effective sentence. Therefore, many students who have a good command of English grammar do not know how to write effective sentences. This is partly because effective sentences require unity, coherence, consistency, conciseness and variety.

1. Unity

Unity is the first quality of an effective sentence. It means there is only one main idea in a sentence and that idea is complete. In other words, every word or phrase in the sentence should contribute to making one clear idea. For example:

(1) We paid a porter two dollars for taking our luggage to our rooms, and the hotel lobby was very elegant.

> We paid a porter two dollars for taking our luggage to our rooms. We found that the hotel lobby was very elegant. (improved)

(2) Luxun wrote many famous novels and essays and died in 1936.

> Luxun, who wrote many famous novels and essays, died in 1936. (improved)

2. Coherence

Coherence means clear and correct arrangement of the parts of a sentence. To achieve coherence, we can resort to a parallelism and subordination, and keep consistency in voice, mood and person.

1) Parallelism

Parallelism is achieved by balancing word against word, clause against clause. It helps clarify the relationship between a writer's parallel ideas, or between the parallel parts of a single idea. Here are two ways of achieving parallelism.

(1) Join elements by using coordinating conjunctions. For example:

> On Sunday afternoon, I like having a glass of tea and reading an interesting novel.
>
> It is said that there is going to be a thunderstorm and that we'd better stay at home.

(2) Join elements by using correlative conjunctions. For example:

> Bill Gates is *not only* a soft ware developer *but also* an idol of young people.
>
> *Both* the catalogue *and* the price-list are enclosed for your convenience.

2) Subordination

Subordination is a non-parallel and non-symmetrical relation between two clauses in such a way that one is a part of the other. Correct use of subordination helps clarify the relationship between ideas. For example:

Many people exercise every day and never lose weight. *While* exercising is important, the only way to lose weight is to stop eating too much.

3. Consistency

A well written sentence needs to keep consistency in person and number, tense, voice and mood. Any unnecessary shifts will lead to awkward or ineffective sentences. Here are some examples in terms of consistency.

If *a student* does not understand a problem, *he or she* should consult the instructor.

For years I have been *attending* summer camp and *enjoying* every minute of it.

They insisted that the money *be collected* and that a receipt *be given* in return.

The Asia Company *painted* the house, *and remodeled* the kitchen.

After *the boy* locked the door, *he* remembered that he had left his key in the room.

4. Conciseness

Conciseness refers to the absence of redundant words in writing. A good sentence should avoid using such words. As long as the meaning of a sentence is clear, we should cut out as many words as possible. Look at the following examples.

(1) Wordy: The chairman of the board will give up his job next year because of old age.

Concise: The chairman of the board will retire next year.

(2) Wordy: The woman who is dressed in black over there is the person who is now in charge of our sales department.

Concise: The woman in black over there is the manager of our sales department.

5. Variety

Variety refers to the mixture of different sentence structures. A composition will seem rather dull if it consists only of short or long sentences. Dullness will not be able to arouse the readers' interest either if all the sentences are loose or periodic sentences.

1) Beginnings of sentences

Most English sentences begin with the subject. However, a composition would seem boring if several consecutive sentences begin in the same way. The following are several different ways to begin a sentence.

Cold and hungry, he can hardly go to sleep.

Reluctantly the children turned off TV and went to bed.

To complete the bridge before the National Day, the whole staff worked all day and all night.

When he was only five years old, he wrote his first poem.

Who will attend the meeting for the Notification of Award of the bidding has not been decided yet.

The world's second largest country in land size, Canada stretches 3222 miles from east to west.

2) Sentence structure

Sentences are classified according to the number and kind of clauses within them. The four basic kinds of sentences are simple, compound, complex and compound-complex. To make them more interesting, we should vary the types of sentences.

Jason and Luis finished their work and went home.

Penguins cannot fly, but they can dive into the ocean.

Football is an autumn sport; baseball is a spring sport.

I enjoy a comedy more than I enjoy heavy drama.

Although I have tried many times, tennis is one sport that I cannot master.

3) Long and short sentences

Sentence length is also an important factor. Good writing uses a mixture of short and long sentences, for both short and long sentences have their own functions. On the one hand, short sentences are clear and straightforward. On the other hand, long sentences are widely used in describing details or making explanations. Your compositions will sound more pleasant if you vary the length of sentences. For example:

(1) He is our monitor. He sits beside me. He works hard. He likes to help others. He is the best student in our class. He often gets praises from the teachers.

The boy *who* sits beside me is our monitor. He *not only* works hard *but also* likes to help others. *As* the best student in our class, he often gets praises from the teachers. (improved)

(2) I want to meet you and your directors. I have long been looking forward to the opportunity. I may be able to hold a friendly talk with you.

The opportunity to meet you and your directors is something *that* I have long been looking forward to, *and* I can only hope now *that* some day I may be able to hold a friendly talk with you. (improved)

IV. Five Steps for Business Writing

Generally speaking, the business writing process is made up of preparing, formatting, organizing, drafting and revising.

1. Preparing

As is known to all, preparing to write involves making it clear about the objective, the reader and the scope of writing.

The objective is the purpose of writing, which needs to be specific and detailed. Otherwise, it will be difficult for the reader to get the main ideas of the document.

The reader of a business text can be a colleague in the company, a new customer or supplier in the market. And a careful reader analysis is helpful to achieving the writing objective.

The scope of the writing refers to the kind and amount of information for the reader to understand the objective. It should be based on who the reader is and what relationship lies between the reader and the writing topic.

2. Formatting

Formatting refers to choosing format or layout of the business text. It aims at choosing the right way of presenting the document, making the document more interesting. The former picks up a physical look that makes one type of document different from another. The latter decides on fonts, spaces and margins. A good format is to arouse readers' interest.

3. Organizing

Organizing deals with gathering information, sorting details and making an outline. Information can be gathered from other people, from the documents available or from the Internet. Then the writer needs to sift the details and manage to make an outline for the business text.

4. Drafting

Now that the outline is ready, the writer can begin to write the first draft. The following are some practical tips on how to draft. The first draft can be written as complete as possible. Thus, during revision it will be easy to cut out material than to look for more in order to meet the requirements of length of the text. In drafting the business text, a writer needs to leave both margin and enough space between lines for further adding information or inserting correction.

5. Revising

Revising is to turn the draft into a finished product. It deals with more than editing and proofreading in terms of format or language. A check on the overall tone is also necessary based on a careful reader analysis. After you have carefully revised the draft item by item, you are ready to make a clean final copy.

Part II Displaying Your Prowess Fully

I. Complete the following sentences with the words and expressions given below.

(1) is/maintain/and/it/important/marketing promotions/both/high quality/to/of/products/to/boost

_____

(2) we/form/comparing/finally/the error/figures/in/four sources/discovered/the sheet

_____

(3) I/too/we/think/the/price/the trucks/will/is/have to/high/pay for

_____

(4) scheduled/was/owing to/the convention/for/canceled/travel/January/restrictions

(5) we/that/experienced and creative/has/Mr. Jones/an opportunity/are/to advance/sure/ in the company

II. Complete the following sentences with the appropriate forms of the given words.

(1) Smoking cigarettes (be) _____ dangerous to your health.

(2) What he wanted to know (be) _____ the pay, the living and working conditions, and the kind of job he would be assigned.

(3) This was the (decision) _____ factor to our success.

(4) The position is (adapt) _____ to his ability.

(5) The committee is (make) _____ up of eight people.

(6) This work order must (complete) _____ by Friday; therefore you may have to work late or Thursday.

(7) The newspaper (publish) _____ in Los Angeles carried the story of the merger.

(8) The board meeting (hold) _____ next Friday will be critical to the company.

III. Correct the following sentence fragments or run-on sentences.

(1) Take the money back. I don't want.

(2) Bill asked for a loan. Which he promised to pay back in two years.

(3) Several textile firms have to close down, therefore there was widespread unemployment in these areas.

(4) The heat was up to 40℃ in the apartment the air was so dry that the skin felt parched.

(5) Smokers claim the right to smoke in public places. While non-smokers claim the right to clean air.

IV. Combine each set of the following sentences into one sentence by either coordination or subordination.

(1) The manual will contain 266 pages. The manual will be sold to the franchises at $2 a book. The price is about half the actual production and distribution cost.

(2) Many of the college's early graduates became ministers in the Puritan congregations throughout New England. The college never formally affiliated with any specific religious denomination.

(3) UNDP(The United Nations Development Programme) was prepared to respond to

emergency needs as they arose. His delegation welcomed it. The basically long-term operations that characterized those programs.

(4) We are the leading bicycle dealers in this district. Cycling is popular in this district. We have branches in three neighboring countries.

(5) You would effect shipment as soon as possible. We should be very much obliged. We enable the buyers to catch the brisk demand at the start of the season.

V. Rearrange the following sentences to form an effective paragraph.

(1) Different habits and culture tradition often make you lose your head and balance.

(2) In this way you have a lot of interesting experiences.

(3) On the whole, attending a foreign college is charming and nice.

(4) Of course, most of these problems are due to lack of experience.

(5) Moreover, you can improve your second language with ease.

(6) You can gradually become accustomed to them.

(7) However, you should also find that there are a lot of barriers lying ahead.

(8) Studying in a foreign country enlarges your field of vision by looking at your own country from outside.

(9) With the development of our reform, the opportunities to go abroad are increasing and whether to attend a foreign college or university becomes a hot issue.